C0-DXD-003

SEEKING GOD

AN INVESTIGATIVE JOURNEY

SEEKING GOD: AN INVESTIGATIVE JOURNEY

Copyright © 2012 Chris Norman

All rights reserved. No part of this book may be reproduced in any manner whatsoever without prior written permission from the publisher, except where noted in the text and in the case of brief quotations embodied in critical articles and reviews.

Credits

Author: Chris Norman

Designed by Josh VonGunten; Michael Bianski

Unless otherwise indicated, all Scripture quotations are taken from the HOLY BIBLE, NEW INTERNATIONAL VERSION®. Copyright © 1973, 1978, 1984 by International Bible Society. Used by permission of Zondervan Publishing House. All rights reserved.

ISBN 978-0-615-39375-9

Printed in the United States of America

ACKNOWLEDGEMENTS

I want to thank several people, beyond my family and my church, whose influence has been significant in this book. My first pastor in Ann Arbor, Michigan, Wes Rowe, wrote an investigative study for seekers, and this was my first exposure to this style of writing. I had an instructor named D.A. Carson during my doctoral studies at Trinity University who taught me how to engage the postmodern mind and yet retain historic Christian truth. Alan Hirsch taught me that Jesus' mission needs a church more than a church needs a mission. Neil Cole's influence has emphasized that mission communities should be simple and easily reproducible. Paul Maconochie taught me the balance of Word and Spirit and how restoration is holistic. Mike Breen has shown me the dominant themes of covenant and kingdom and how they are woven throughout all of Scripture. These leaders, and many others, have impacted my theology and my life in meaningful ways.

I also want to thank several people who invested directly in this book through feedback and editing: Ben Sternke, Lindsay Hotmire, Scott Jester, John Haydock, Tim Smith, Andy Booth, Josh VonGunten, Giovana Cavarretta, Orville Erickson, and Tara Riehm.

My ultimate thanks goes to Jesus who is the true inspiration of all that is written.

—Chris Norman

CONTENTS

CHAPTER ONE: THE BEGINNING — ASTONISHING PARADISE   1
    What if you were there at the beginning?
    If there is a God, what is he like?
    Me, represent God on this earth?
    Are you ready to be personally interviewed?
    Paradise in the Garden

CHAPTER TWO: A KINGDOM OF EVIL IS ESTABLISHED IN THE WORLD   12
    There is an unseen world around us
    A ringleader named Satan takes center stage
    Everyone has messed up in life
    Our bad choices come from deep within our hearts
    Where will my soul go when I die?
    The dominant kingdom today is Satan's

CHAPTER THREE: GOD BUILDS A FAMILY, BUT SOMETHING'S NOT RIGHT   24
    Satan's Kingdom advancing
    A snapshot of the Old Testament
    The first example of spiritual conversion
    Whose kingdom did your family advance growing up?

CHAPTER FOUR: THE MODEL RELATIONSHIP — JESUS AND HIS FATHER   37
    Jesus is introduced as God's son
    Jesus teaches a new way of Life
    God wants to adopt you into his family
    God wants to give you a new identity
    God is ready to welcome you home with open arms

CHAPTER FIVE: THE CALL TO GIVE UP EVERYTHING AND FOLLOW JESUS 50
    Jesus goes to the cross
    Jesus' message: a life change toward God
    Faith isn't blind but reasonable
    There is no magical prayer to receive forgiveness
    How do I really know if I am a follower of Jesus?
    Your Faith Journey

CHAPTER SIX: THE MISSION OF BRINGING HEAVEN TO EARTH 63
    Our mission – reverse the effects of sin
    Paradise will once again return on a new earth
    Bringing heaven to earth by the power of the Spirit
    Jesus hands off the baton to the early church
    What is the church and what's the point?

CHAPTER SEVEN: A NEW PATH TO LIFE 76
    The Bible is your anchor of truth
    The Holy Spirit empowers you
    Balancing your identity and your activity
    The impact of mentoring
    Becoming a part of a community on a mission

INTRODUCTION

Most people in the world are on some type of spiritual journey, and often, our journeys involve many unanswered questions. We want to know what purpose we have in life, and we want to find answers to our most significant questions.

> Who am I?
> What is the point of life?
> Who is God?
> Does God even exist?
> What happens when people die?
> If God is good, why do bad things happen?
> Don't all religions in the world lead to God or a supreme being?
> Where do I go if I want something more than just another religion?
> How did my life turn out like this?

Over the next seven weeks, we will walk through a journey that could be life changing for you. Wrestling through difficult questions like these is a good and healthy part of the process.

NO ASSUMPTIONS YOU BELIEVE THE BIBLE IS TRUE

The purpose of this journey is to equip you to investigate the claims Jesus and the Bible make about the past, the present, and the future. Its primary intent is to help you discover how you fit into God's plan for the world. If it is true that God created you, and if it is true that this God is a heavenly Father who loves you and desires a close relationship with you, seeking Him is the best place to find true love and peace in life. This study does not assume you believe these things, or that you believe the Bible is true, or that you even know anything about the Bible or God.

These chapters will reveal what the Bible claims about these important life questions, and then you can decide whether you believe those claims or not. Instead of simply knowing what a church teaches, what a specific denomination believes, or what a certain leader says, this study asks you to find passages in the Bible yourself so that you can come to your own conclusions.

How do I fit into the overall storyline of the Bible and the world? People who have spent time studying the Bible have often studied it topically (e.g. finding passages about forgiveness, peace, heaven, God's love) or perhaps simply read parts of the Bible randomly. Many people, however, have never understood how the Bible fits together as a progressive story from beginning to end, and how we fit into this story today. Once we understand this, however, it is life-changing. So even if this is not your first time participating in a Bible study, perhaps you will see the Bible as a story for the first time in your life.

DIFFERENCE BETWEEN OLD TESTAMENT AND NEW TESTAMENT

The Bible has two main sections. They are called "testaments" or "covenants," which simply means agreements or contracts. The basic difference between the Old and New Testament is that the Old was written before Jesus, and the New was written after Jesus. What we will see is that God has a master plan for the world, from beginning to end, and he has implemented his plan in two different phases, signified by the Old and New Testaments.

WHAT KIND OF BIBLE SHOULD I USE?

A widely used translation is the New International Version (NIV), and we recommend you use this version, but any modern English translation will be fine. You can also view multiple translations online at biblegateway.com.

HOW TO LOOK UP VERSES

When you go through each lesson, you will be asked to find verses in your Bible. If you look in your table of contents at the beginning of your Bible, you will see books divided between the Old and New Testaments. There are 39 books in the Old Testament (OT) and 27 books listed in the New Testament (NT). In order to help assist you as you find verses, each reference will have OT or NT next to it. For example, Matthew 7:12 (NT) means the verse is in the New Testament, the book of Matthew, chapter seven, and verse 12. The large numbers in your Bible are the chapters, and small numbers are the verses.

INTERACTING WITH YOUR STUDY PARTNER

More than likely, you are going through this study because someone invited you to do it with them. The best way to go through this book is to have each lesson done ahead of time, and then meet with someone once a week for 60-90 minutes to go through it together (one-on-one or couple-with-couple). It is intended to be interactive and discussion-generating!

JOURNAL YOUR THOUGHTS AND QUESTIONS

At the end of every chapter is a place for you to write down some questions that the material caused you to consider. This space can also be used to simply journal some reflections on what you read, what you think, or how you feel. Perhaps you were greatly impacted by something specific. Write this down. Later you can go back and read about things you wrestled with or ways in which you were moved in your heart.

ARE YOU READY FOR THE JOURNEY?

No matter where you're at in life, the content of these lessons will challenge you, encourage you, and inspire you in ways you may not expect. Maybe you are a new follower of Christ, and you are using this study to help you become more grounded in your faith. Maybe you are unsure about all this "God stuff" and want to find out what the Bible actually says about life. No matter where you're coming from, your openness and honesty will be your greatest contribution. Whether you believe God is real or not, the Bible says he will begin to reveal himself to you as you seek him. Going through this study might be a life-changing exercise for you. Blessings to you on your journey of seeking God!

"You will seek me and find me when you seek me with all your heart." (Jeremiah 29:13)

CHAPTER ONE

THE BEGINNING: ASTONISHING PARADISE

I studied philosophy during my years in college. Philosophy is one of those subjects: you either love it or hate it. I was part of the "love it" crowd. Asking life's deepest questions had always been appealing to me, even though I didn't have many answers.

As I started to study philosophy of religion, I began a quest of seeking a supreme being. Even though I didn't grow up in church and had never read the Bible, I was always intrigued by the Bible and the other major religions in the world. During my sophomore year in college, I spent two semesters in London as a foreign exchange student. My goal was to study philosophy in a different culture and expand my horizons. I can clearly remember the day that my perspective began to widen. One of my professors asked if I was a Christian. I stood there, looked at her for a few seconds, and said, "Well, uh... hmm... I don't think so... maybe." I had a general belief in God, but I really didn't know what to say.

One of my drinking and drug buddies from high school began following Jesus during my freshman year in college. He seemed to jump in with both feet. His journey was much quicker than mine. After he started following Jesus, he would talk to me and write letters to me trying to get me to experience some of the ways he found God. I just figured he was going through a phase, and I had no interest in becoming some "religious freak."

As I was studying various religions, I also decided to attend some church gatherings and interview some of the leaders. I met with one church leader in London who said to me, "You are asking great questions, but you are also very young. You have your entire life to figure out answers. Take your time, and don't be in too much of a hurry." I took his advice for about twenty-four hours, and then I was back on my quest for answers. I felt the need to make some kind of conclusion for or against this whole "God thing."

This book is for others who seem to be on this quest of seeking God or some kind of Supreme Being as well. Maybe you don't even know how to describe your quest, but you know there has to be more to life than what you see around you. Sometimes it is exciting to seek answers to life's most difficult questions, and other times it is frustrating and confusing. In the end, though, the pursuit is worth it.

WHAT YOU WILL LEARN IN THIS CHAPTER:

God is the creator of everything. He reveals himself as one who is perfect and different than anything else he has created, but he is also one who is loving and personal. God created human beings to have a special role in his creation, and he desires them to represent him on the earth by taking care of everything he created. Initially, the first two humans, Adam and Eve, had a close relationship with God and took care of the Earth.

WHAT IF YOU WERE THERE AT THE BEGINNING?

Think about what you appreciate most about the beauty of the world. Maybe it is the Grand Canyon, the Amazon rainforest, the beauty of the ocean, or the radiance of the moon and stars. The Bible teaches that God is a personal being and created everything we see (Genesis 1:1). Can you imagine what it would have been like to witness God creating the world? What an experience you could tell your friends and family. God created a universe and then created multiple galaxies within this universe. Within one particular galaxy, later called the Milky Way, God created several planets. And on this one particular planet, later called Earth, God created life.

God created plant life, insect life, animal life, and human life. Why do you think God chose to create life?

1. Read Psalm 139:1-18. Why do you think God created you, and what feelings do you think he has for you?

....

....

....

....

....

GOD DESIRES A RELATIONSHIP WITH YOU

When God created life, he did not create all of life in the exact same way. When he created human life, he did something unique. He created man and woman in his own likeness and image.

2. Record what Genesis 1:27 (OT) says about God's image:

....

....

....

When man and woman were created in God's image and likeness, they were created with a unique ability to relate to God unlike anything else in all creation. Man and woman would be able to reason, be self aware, communicate feelings, have a will to make independent decisions, show love, grant forgiveness, and demonstrate many other traits that are similar to God. While dirt, trees, insects, animals, the moon, stars, and everything else God created should be appreciated and cared for, God created man and woman with the ability to relate to him unlike anything else.

Because these God-like traits were given to humans, God interacted with them differently than the rest of his creation. Right from the beginning, God communicated to humans, and they communicated back to him. In other words, because they were created in his image, God had a relationship with them.

This concept of relationship is a dominant theme throughout the Bible and will be one of two major themes as we move forward on this spiritual journey.

IF THERE IS A GOD, WHAT IS HE LIKE?

As we go forward in this study, we need to ask ourselves, "If there is a God who created everything and desires a relationship with us, what is he like?"

What we believe about God forms an important foundation in our lives. Some people believe God is a strict authority figure who is always angry and ready to zap people the moment they step out of line. Others believe God is like an easy-going grandfather who simply loves and accepts everyone regardless of how they live or what they believe. Others think God is distant and cannot be bothered by the details of our lives. All of these perspectives affect the way people live and relate to God.

THE FOUNDATION OF GOD'S CHARACTER

GOD IS HOLY, PURE, AND UNIQUE — BALANCE OF BOTH — GOD IS LOVING, MERCIFUL, AND COMPASSIONATE

3. Which do you think most resembles your view of God, and why? 1) a strict authority figure, 2) a loving grandfather, or 3) one who is distant?

....

....

....

....

....

....

While no list of attributes or characteristics could fully describe God, from the Bible's perspective there are two traits that are foundational to all others: God's holiness and God's love.

The word holy has two primary meanings: 1) morally pure, 2) different and unique (Psalm 29:2, 93:5, Ezekiel 36:23, Isaiah 29:23). The Bible says God is 100% pure. He has never had a bad thought or an ulterior motive. He has never made a mistake. To say God is holy also means he is different from everything else in the world. He made humans like him in many ways, but all of us are still limited and prone to error.

Because of this, there are certain aspects of God that we will never understand. If you have a hard time understanding every detail of God or why he would do or allow certain things in this life, you are not alone. None of us can fully comprehend God because he is holy.

The other foundational attribute of God is his unconditional love (Psalm 51:1, Psalm 103:11, Luke 3:22, 1 John 4:16). God is forgiving, compassionate, patient, gentle, and merciful. He is spoken of as "Father" in the Bible and takes a parental role to those in relationship with him (Matt. 6:1, Matt. 7:11). God desires to bless, protect, and provide for his people because he is a God of love.

So from the Bible's perspective, God is holy, powerful, and altogether different from us. However, he is also compassionate, merciful and loving toward us.

THE POWER OF A FAMILY COMMUNITY

Read through Genesis 2:15-18. Not only did God create man and woman for the purpose of relating to him and interacting with him within a relationship, he also created two genders for the purpose of relating to one another and interacting together in relationship.

4. According to Genesis 2:18 (OT), why did God create two genders in the human race and not just one?

....

....

....

....

....

Personal Story from Author:
I will never forget when I met my wife for the first time in college. The more

we began to communicate, the more emotion and feeling we developed for each other. The more feelings we developed for each other, the more we wanted to communicate. We would study in the library together; we would eat lunch in the cafeteria together; we would attend sporting events together; we would hang out together; and then at night, we would talk on the phone for hours. Because we were developing a closer relationship together, we longed to spend more time together. With communication and time together, our relationship was deepening.

The human dynamic of relationship and communication is the reason God chose to create us in his image. Not only can we have a close and loving relationship with one another, but we can have this kind of relationship with God as well. Have you ever had an experience of longing for God like you would long for someone you love here on earth?

God created two genders because he wanted to build a family on the earth who would live together in relationship with each other and God. This is why he would eventually tell Adam and Eve to bear children. God's desire is to be in relationship with a family of people on earth.

DISCUSS IT TOGETHER

Spend a few moments with your study partner and discuss a relationship you have with someone that is healthy, and then, describe one that is unhealthy. Afterwards, discuss the similarities this might have as you relate to God. Is your relationship with God healthy or unhealthy?

ME, REPRESENT GOD ON THIS EARTH?

Not only did God create humans for the purpose of relationship, but he also gave them the responsibility to care for the earth he created. He did not put the trees, the sun, the animals, or even the angels in charge. From the Bible's perspective, God has made his desire crystal clear: humans are his representatives on earth.

5. Record Genesis 1:28 (OT).

....

....

....

We mentioned that relationship would be one of the two major themes in this study. Responsibility is the other major theme we will see as we move forward. As we take care of God's creation, we are representing him and caring for his creation on his behalf.

A Skeptic's View:

I do believe in a God, but I feel like I have more questions than I have answers. Some people act like they know everything they need to know about God and they quote all these different Bible verses to prove their answers. The problem I see is that most of these people don't live up to what they preach and teach. I have this one co-worker who seems really religious and seems to be a big church-goer, but he is the most uncompassionate person in our entire department. Just the other day, we all chipped in money to help a recent employee who got laid off. Not only did this guy not contribute anything to this person in need, he claimed he had to go to a church service the night we all helped this single mom move into a different apartment. I don't get it - you go to a church service that teaches the importance of helping people in need instead of actually helping someone who has a need? This is one of the reasons I don't believe in organized religion - too much hypocrisy.

ARE YOU READY TO BE PERSONALLY INTERVIEWED?

Imagine you are being interviewed by a reporter. This reporter is asking you several questions about your family, your job, interests, and hobbies. The reporter shifts gears and says, "This next set of questions will revolve around your understanding and beliefs about God." How would you answer the following questions?

6. Can you name a significant event or circumstance in your life that has shaped your understanding of who God is (either positively or negatively)?

....
....
....
....
....

7. Did you grow up believing in God, and is your belief any different today than it was growing up?

....

....

....

....

8. Do you think that some of your beliefs about God could be right and some of them could be wrong? If so, how would you go about discovering which are right and which are wrong?

....

....

....

....

....

WHY DO YOU BELIEVE THE THINGS YOU BELIEVE?

Many people form their beliefs from one of four sources of authority: reason, experience, tradition, or the Bible. We often use multiple sources to develop our knowledge of life. However, when two or more sources contradict each other, everyone has one source that takes precedence over the others. For example, the Bible says that Jesus walked on water; reason says this defies gravity; experience says I have never seen anyone do that, and tradition says it has never historically happened. In this example, one source contradicts the other three. Whenever this happens, and it happens more often than most people realize, your conclusion regarding what you believe indicates your final source of authority.

9. Of the four sources of authority (reason, experience, tradition, Bible), which source do you think you use as your final source of authority in life?

....

10. How do you think that source will affect or possibly limit your pursuit of God?

....

....

....

....

In today's world we often hear people say things like, "It is okay for you to believe those things, and for you they are true. For me, however, I have my own beliefs about what is true. I am not saying you are wrong, but don't say I am wrong either." This is called relativism. Within this philosophy of thinking, everyone has their own beliefs, and nobody can say who's right or who's wrong. With this mentality, there are no absolutes in life.

Go back to the illustration of the Bible stating that Jesus walked on water. Some people, who believe in the Bible, believe this happened. Others, who may have a different source of authority, do not believe this happened. Can both be right? Relativism says it is judgmental to say some people's beliefs are right and others are wrong. It is really the easy way out: "everyone is correct and no one has a right to tell me my beliefs are wrong." Relativism has distorted our ability to think clearly and make real sense out of our world. The fact is that Jesus either did walk on water or he didn't. Both people cannot be right; therefore, one belief is right and the other belief is wrong, regardless of how sincerely the person believes it.

11. How do you think relativism, as it pertains to morals, has affected the way you think and the way you live?

....

....

....

....

....

PARADISE IN THE GARDEN OF EDEN

The first chapter of Genesis gives a broad overview of everything God created. Adam and Eve were unified together; they represented God on the earth by taking care of the Garden of Eden. They had a healthy and loving relationship with their creator. God would talk with them, and they would talk with him. Whatever he said, they believed. He loved them, and they loved him. They lived with no pain, no trouble, no arguments, no dishonesty, no wrong motives, no skepticism, no arrogance, no selfishness, no injuries, no disease, no sicknesses, no handicaps, no disobedience, no death, and no sin. It was paradise.

12. As you observe pain, heartache, trouble, and tragedy in this life, does it give you any encouragement knowing the world wasn't like this from the beginning when God created it? Knowing that God created a world that was a paradise, what does this tell you about who God is and what he is like?

....
....
....
....

CHAPTER SUMMARY

Our desire is to understand God, the world, and how we fit into God's overall plan. To do this, it is important for us to learn how God originally created things and his intention for life. Out of God's holiness and love, he created a beautiful world. Like any loving parent, his crowning achievement was found in the creation of his children – a man and woman created in his image. As they built his family upon the earth, he longed to commune with them in relationship.

God also gave this man and woman the responsibility to represent him on the earth and to take care of the creation he made on his behalf. They were to live in perfect community together, and God was to be at the center of their lives. This actually happened in the Garden of Eden. For a brief time in earth's history, a time of peace and prosperity actually existed; it was a time when everything was just as God planned.

In the next chapter, we will see what went wrong. Before focusing on the problems, it is encouraging to see what was intended. It is the most incredible picture you could ever imagine! This beautiful reality of paradise will play a role later in this study as we find out God's plan to restore his creation back to its original and intended beauty and wholeness.

QUESTIONS OR JOURNAL REFLECTIONS

CHAPTER TWO

A KINGDOM OF EVIL IS ESTABLISHED IN THE WORLD

In my pursuit of seeking God, one of my biggest obstacles was all the pre-conceived beliefs I had about God, the church, and the Bible. I remember one day debating a campus pastor between classes. I said to him, "All Christians are hypocrites; being a part of a church community isn't important when following God; the Bible is full of errors; Jesus isn't the only way to God…"

I believed these things with conviction, even though I had never fully examined them myself. I believed the Bible was narrow-minded, and that anyone who claimed to follow it was narrow-minded as well. This antagonism was deep-seated, but at the same time, a spiritual curiosity was growing within me.

It was during my time in London, however, that I began to feel a tug of war in my spirit. On some days, I was open to God's prompting in my life. I began to believe that maybe he was revealing himself to me, maybe he did care, and maybe I could know him in a personal way. On other days, I wanted nothing to do with God and was content with my own life.

While all this was happening, I remember telling a friend, "There is no such thing as Satan, a devil, or demons. These are just symbolic ideas representing the bad things that happen in life." I was about to learn there was more going on, however, regarding my antagonistic feelings than I was aware. I was in a spiritual battle and didn't even know it.

WHAT YOU WILL LEARN IN THIS CHAPTER

Adam and Eve enjoyed paradise with God for a time, but a spirit being called Satan wanted to destroy God's relationship with his people. From the moment God cast Satan out of Heaven, Satan has been lying about the very nature of God (Genesis 3:4-5, John 8:44) and influencing others to believe these lies. Satan enticed Adam and Eve to question God and turn against him. They succumbed to the temptation, and their relationship with God was destroyed. This affected everything from that point forward. No longer did humans have a close relationship with God, and no longer did they authentically represent him on the earth. From this point forward, Satan began using the human race to build his own kingdom on the earth.

THERE IS AN UNSEEN WORLD AROUND US

According to the Bible, God not only created everything we see, but he also created many things we cannot see—a spiritual world. This spiritual reality is expressed in two ways: 1) God created a spiritual aspect to every human: a soul, and 2) God created spiritual beings called angels.

Genesis 1 and 2 are a summary and overview of everything God created. However, this account was never intended to be an exhaustive historical description of every event in creation. For example, God created angels, but we are not told exactly when he created them. Also, before Satan enters the Garden in Genesis 3, a significant event occurs that is not recorded anywhere in Genesis: the rebellion of many angels against God, which is indicated in other parts of the Bible.

FREEDOM TO CHOOSE GOOD OR EVIL

God created both humans and angels with the capacity to make moral decisions (either good or bad). Many of God's angels today are involved in the lives of God's people in a positive way (Hebrews 1:14, 13:2, Revelation. 5:11-12, 22:6). Some angels, however, decided to use their free will to turn against God. They wanted God's power, and so they chose to rebel against him.

Even today, a battle between good and evil is being fought in the world. It is not hard to observe this battle because we see it everywhere.

1. Read Ezekiel 28:13-16 (OT) or Isaiah 14:12-15 (OT). According to the two passages that allude to Satan's fall from heaven, what led to his judgment from God?

....

....

....

....

....

2. Read 2 Peter 2:4 (NT) and Jude 6 (NT). What did God do to the angels who chose Satan's plan over God's?

....

....

....

....

A RINGLEADER NAMED SATAN TAKES CENTER STAGE

There was one angel in particular who decided he wanted to be like God and build his own kingdom in the heavenly realm. He is called Satan, Lucifer, or the Devil. He turned against God, enticing many other angels to follow him in his rebellion, and he launched an attack against God and the rest of his angels. Satan, a created being, was no match for the eternal creator, and in judgment, God threw him and his angelic followers out of heaven and down to earth. These fallen angels, also called demons, opposed everything God stood for and were led by their powerful ringleader Satan.

Satan's attempted rebellion failed, but he had not given up. He made another attempt at building a kingdom set against God, this time not in the heavens but on the earth. His new strategy was to entice God's most prized creation, human beings, to follow him instead of God. Satan hates everything God loves (2 Cor. 11:4, I Peter 5:8), so his predominant goal is to break God's relationship with his people. He made his way to the Garden of Eden where Adam and Eve were enjoying paradise. As we recall from the previous chapter, they enjoyed perfect community together, and were in a perfect relationship of love with God.

3. Read through Genesis 3:1-7 (OT). Although Satan was successful in enticing them to evil, how were Adam and Eve responsible for their own actions?

....

....

....

GOD'S DESIRE FOR CLOSE RELATIONSHIP NOW IN JEOPARDY

Though Satan was unsuccessful at establishing his kingdom in the heavens, his plan on earth was succeeding. He had tempted Adam and Eve to sin, breaking their perfect relationship with God. Sin is any thought, word, or action that goes against God's will and desire for us. It is anything we do that damages our relationship with God. Not only did their sin break their relationship with God personally, they would now pass a sinful nature to their children as well (Rom. 5:12). God clearly outlined the consequences of disobedience. "You will surely die" (Genesis 2:17). God's perfect paradise had now been corrupted by sin and death. Death, the ultimate expression of separation from God, came to earth when Adam and Eve sinned and can be understood in three ways.

<u>Spiritual death</u>: Man now has a sinful nature, is separated from God spiritually, and is prone to disobey God simply as a way of life (Rom. 3:9-18).

<u>Physical death</u>: Man will now only live a short time on the earth (not forever). His body will decay, be susceptible to disease, and his soul will be separated from his body at death (2 Cor. 5:6-7).

<u>Eternal death</u>: Because of spiritual death and eventual physical death, the

ultimate consequence of sin is a permanent separation from God in an eternal place of punishment (2 Thes. 1:9).

Because every person on the earth is a descendant of Adam and Eve, everyone since then has been born with a broken relationship with God and a sinful nature that is prone to disobedience. This is why no one needs to teach a toddler how to lie, use violence to get his way, or be selfish. These things come naturally because of a child's sinful nature. From very early on, parenting is about helping kids make choices against their natural desires. It is about teaching children to choose kindness over selfishness, truth over lies, God's kingdom over Satan's.

4. According to the content of this chapter thus far, explain in your own words why everyone comes into the world with a sinful nature, and why no one on the face of the earth has the ability to live a morally perfect life without sin. And secondly, do you believe this is true?

....

....

....

....

....

A Skeptic's View:

One of the things I don't like about church is that it seems to have such a negative message all the time. Don't do this, don't do that, God will judge you if you behave this way, etc. I have enough negativity in my life. I don't need someone else to tell me how wrong I am, or that if I died today I would go to hell. I may not be perfect, but I surely have done nothing worthy of hell. In fact, I am not really sure I believe in a literal hell. Could it really be worse than what some people experience here on earth? What I need in my life is a positive environment. I don't need to hear about sin, judgment, and hell. I think the positive message from religion is the idea of loving people and treating others as you want to be treated. I think any religion in the world or any church that helps people love others on our planet is doing a good thing and making a positive contribution in our society. I want to see the church have a more positive message. Just show me how I can be a better person and live a happier life.

EVERYONE HAS MESSED UP IN LIFE

We all know that no one is perfect and that we all sin, but why is that? Why do we keep making the same mistakes? Why are we selfish? Why do we have thoughts we are glad no one can hear? These are important questions to ask during our journey. God loves honest questions and our willingness to be open and vulnerable about our shortcomings. All throughout the Bible, we see his willingness to reach out to those who have messed up their lives. We do a lot of positive things in the world, but we also do a lot of things that are wrong. We need to come to terms with our mistakes and sins, acknowledge them for what they are, understand the root cause of our negative behavior, and then attempt to do what we can to change our lives the way God desires.

5. Here is a helpful exercise to be real and authentic with your study partner. Write down some sinful decisions you have made in your life and things you have done wrong that you now regret (I John 1:9). Don't be embarrassed. Just be honest:

....

....

....

....

....

....

....

....

....

....

....

....

....

....

DISCUSS IT TOGETHER

Allow your study partner to also share some of his/her sins of the past. Sins are part of our human history and each of our personal stories. It is healthy and cleansing to be open about them.

Personal Story from Author:

I have made plenty of mistakes in my past (particularly before God turned my life around). I drank alcohol excessively, used illegal drugs, was involved in sexual immorality, worked under the table to save on taxes, cheated in school when given the opportunity, lied on an application to get a job, disrespected my parents, shoplifted occasionally, loved sports more than God, was totally consumed with how other people saw me, and the list could go on for awhile! What is interesting is that most people saw me as a pretty normal and comparatively nice guy. What is even more interesting is that none of these things I did ever brought any guilt to my conscience. I did them without any regret. After all, isn't this the way most people live anyway? When we compare ourselves to others, the standard is so low, we often don't even realize how wrong and sinful our lifestyles are.

The first two chapters of Genesis were beautiful, and it was paradise. After Genesis 3, when sin entered the world, chaos and heartache erupted. Adam and Eve hid from God and blamed one another. As they had children and the human race began to populate the earth, we see lying, deceit, immorality, sickness, disease, death, murder, stealing, jealousy, and all the evil that is still evident in our world today. In fact, there is no place on the planet today where these things are absent.

OUR BAD CHOICES COME FROM DEEP WITHIN OUR HEARTS

Often our bad choices are linked to the way we think (Eph. 2:3). Most of our actions, whether good or bad, are preceded by thoughts. Someone disrespects me, I have angry thoughts, and then I yell or say something I later regret. I am attracted to someone; I entertain lustful thoughts, and that can lead to actions I later regret. If I never had a wrong thought, I would never do wrong things. My actions are linked to my thoughts, and my thoughts are linked to my heart, the deepest place of who I am. Therefore, if I want to make a lasting change in my life, something needs to change deep within me. I cannot just try to change my outward behavior or even just my thoughts alone. My goal in seeking God cannot merely be behavior modification but must aim at life transformation. Is it possible that God could do something deep within my heart and being?

6. As you read through Matt. 7:17-27 (NT), what strikes you most about this passage?

....
....
....
....
....
....
....

WHERE WILL MY SOUL GO WHEN I DIE?

Because God has made every person both physically and spiritually, we have a spiritual soul that will live forever. An important question for all of us to consider is whether that soul will be with God forever when it departs from the physical body, or whether that soul will be separated from God in a place called Hell.

7. According to 2 Thessalonians 1:7-9 (NT), whom will God send to hell and how long will it last?

....
....

8. How would you put Matthew 10:28 in your own words?

....
....
....

9. Do you think you have a healthy fear and respect of God, knowing his judgment is eternal? Why or why not?

Although Hell may seem like a place for only evil people, it is a place for anyone who has a broken relationship with God through sin (Matt. 13:49-50). On the other hand, Heaven is a place where there is no evil, rebellion, or sin. Because Heaven is perfect and holy, it is impossible for sinful people to enter without the removal of sin. Jesus came to earth to make forgiveness and removal of sin possible. He did this both to change our future destiny and to show us how to live for God and his kingdom today. We are saved from judgment in the future and saved to a new life of following God today.

What is difficult is that many people don't understand their broken relationship with God and their need for forgiveness. We cannot fix something until we know it is broken. If we are going to have a close relationship with God and know where we fit into his plan for the world, it is essential that we know and recognize what needs to change.

THE DOMINANT KINGDOM TODAY IS SATAN'S

The reason so many people want to make the world a better place is because we witness and see so much pain, heartache, and tragedy.

Everything bad that happens in the world is a facet of Satan's kingdom and sinful choices (Job 1:6-2:10, John 8:44, 16:11, 2 Corinthians 4:4). Satan is the father of sin, and sin is the reason our world is in the shape it's in. Satan's destructive kingdom advances every time we hear about a kidnapping, a murder, an affair, an abortion, a miscarriage, a divorce, a harsh word, a diagnosis of cancer, hateful speech, an incident of racism, death, etc. Some of these things are the direct result of sinful decisions we make, while others are simply the negative results of living in a fallen world. Nonetheless, they are all a part of Satan's destructive kingdom on the earth waging war against God's desire for healthy relationships, harmonious community, physical health, compassion, beauty, and love.

SOMETIMES WE CONTRIBUTE TO SATAN'S KINGDOM

While it may be easy to point the finger at all the evil in the world, we have to come to terms with the fact that at times Satan has used us to advance his kingdom (Matt. 16:23). Every time we lie, erupt in anger, respond without compassion, have a love for money or possessions, are not content, get jealous, are careless about the environment, have lustful thoughts, cheat our employer, don't show God's love to others, refuse to share the gospel with people who need it, or do anything that is not in line with God's perfect character, we not only sin against God, but we advance the wrong kingdom.

10. What are some ways you have consciously or unconsciously helped advance Satan's Kingdom, either by what you have done or what you have not done in life?

....
....
....
....
....

CHAPTER SUMMARY

Because we cannot see the spiritual world, we often forget that life is both physical and spiritual. God created spiritual beings called angels, some of whom were cast out of heaven and became demons. We need to be aware of their influence. It was demonic influence from Satan that led Adam and Eve to sin against God and change the course of human history. Once they sinned against God, everything on the earth changed.

There is now a dominant kingdom on the earth that is advancing, and it's not God's kingdom. Not only did rage, murder, jealousy, lies, wrong motives, disease, and every other expression or consequence of sin enter the world, but the human race died spiritually. God created every human with a spiritual soul that lives forever. Because death entered the world, a human's soul now eventually separates from his body and faces an eternal judgment. Our soul will either spend eternity with God or eternity separated from him. What started out as such a beautiful picture on the earth, as God created everything for his purposes, became a scene of trouble and tragedy. Satan's kingdom is now in full force, and not only do we see his kingdom advancing around us today, but sometimes we even see him using us to do it.

QUESTIONS OR JOURNAL REFLECTIONS

CHAPTER THREE

GOD BUILDS A FAMILY, BUT SOMETHING'S NOT RIGHT

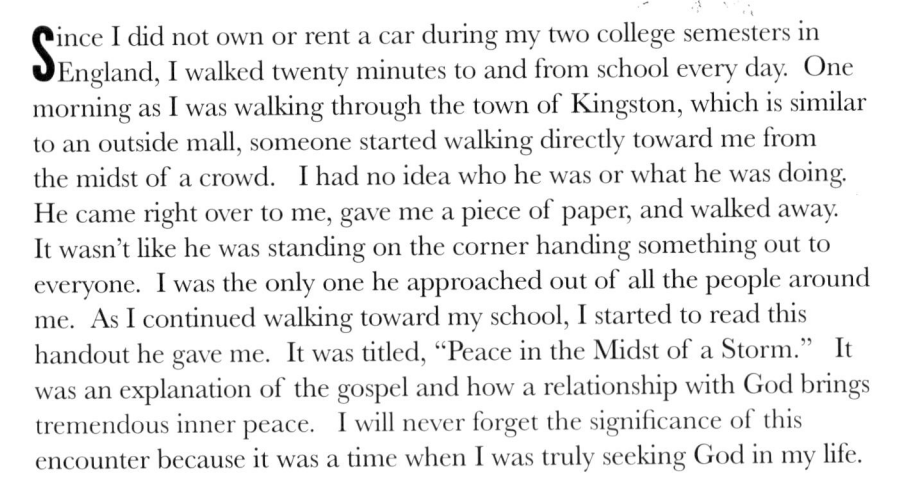

Since I did not own or rent a car during my two college semesters in England, I walked twenty minutes to and from school every day. One morning as I was walking through the town of Kingston, which is similar to an outside mall, someone started walking directly toward me from the midst of a crowd. I had no idea who he was or what he was doing. He came right over to me, gave me a piece of paper, and walked away. It wasn't like he was standing on the corner handing something out to everyone. I was the only one he approached out of all the people around me. As I continued walking toward my school, I started to read this handout he gave me. It was titled, "Peace in the Midst of a Storm." It was an explanation of the gospel and how a relationship with God brings tremendous inner peace. I will never forget the significance of this encounter because it was a time when I was truly seeking God in my life.

While I was overseas, I travelled to fifteen other countries. I spent a week on the Greek Islands. It was the perfect place to contemplate the meaning and origin of life: beautiful cliffs, crashing waves of the Mediterranean Sea, and an unbelievable array of stars at night. Could all of these beautiful surroundings simply be here by chance? God was speaking to me through his creation while I was in Greece.

While in Rome, I went to a church service just for the experience. While I didn't understand anything that was said because it was in Latin, God was speaking to me there as well. His Spirit was prompting me to seek him and search for him.

Whether I was in Greece, Italy, Spain, Morocco, Belgium, France, Switzerland, Germany, the Netherlands, Sweden, or a host of other countries that year, God was everywhere I went, speaking to me and drawing me to him. Everywhere I turned, God was there. This is still true today. While his main activity during Old Testament times was within the nation of Israel, God is at work today everywhere under the sun. God is drawing people to himself all over the planet.

WHAT YOU WILL LEARN IN THIS CHAPTER

Although Satan won over the hearts of the people God created, God had a plan of restoration. He chose a couple, Abraham and Sarah, through which he would begin a new family that would turn away from Satan and back to God. Eventually, this family was called the people of Israel. God was seeking to restore relationship with humanity and enable them to once again represent him on the earth. This representation would not only mean taking care of the earth but also doing battle against the kingdom of Satan.

However, the people of Israel eventually focused too much attention on outward religion without inner devotion; therefore, they struggled to fulfill their calling and often failed. This is a reminder to us of how futile it is to pursue God with outward rituals only. Religion, which is the human attempt to work towards knowing God, can never bring us into a true and loving relationship with him.

SATAN'S KINGDOM ADVANCING

Satan's attempt at building his kingdom on the earth was successful. Due to his influence, everyone is now born with a sinful nature, which means we have a natural tendency to not live for God. We are building Satan's kingdom on the earth when we live this way. As we learned in Chapter Two, we also see the overall consequence of sin in many other ways such as death, disease, genetic disorders, miscarriages, cancer, sickness, injuries, and eternal separation from God in hell. All of these things are aspects of Satan's kingdom and were not a part of God's original plan.

1. What are ways Satan has recently enticed you to sin?

....

....

....

....

2. What are some things you believe about God that might be lies?

....

....

....

....

Man's sin and Satan's progressing kingdom do not take God by surprise. He has a plan that is introduced in Genesis 12 and then carried out through the rest of the Old Testament. The plan was centered on the nation of Israel, which was the family God was creating from the descendants of Abraham and Sarah.

A SNAPSHOT OF THE OLD TESTAMENT

Genesis 1-2 God creates all things; his creation is beautiful, and Adam and Eve live in the perfect community together with God.

Genesis 3 Satan begins building his kingdom on the earth by enticing the parents of the human race to sin against God, and because they did, everything changed.

Genesis 4-11 Satan's kingdom advances; the sin of man becomes more pronounced, and evil and rebellion are widespread on the earth.

Genesis 12 God reveals his plan to restore what was lost back in Genesis 1 and 2. He chooses a couple named Abraham and Sarah to be the first instruments of his plan and to begin a family.

Genesis 12-Malachi The rest of the Old Testament is a record of how those promises to Abraham were mostly fulfilled. However, God's family, Israel, never fully became the people God desired them to be.

GOD PROMISES A NEW FAMILY/NATION IN GENESIS 12

Genesis 12 is a key chapter in the Old Testament. From the moment of the Fall, God desired to establish his own family on the earth that would advance his kingdom over the kingdom of darkness. Relationship and representation were lost in the Garden, so God chose Abraham and Sarah to begin a family that would usher in his Kingdom to the earth. This was a very interesting choice, considering they didn't actually have any kids and were well past the age of child-bearing. If you read through the first seven verses of this chapter, you will notice several promises God gives to Abraham and his wife. Three promises stand out in particular:
- I will form a nation, who will represent me on the earth, from your descendants (Genesis 12:2).
- I will give you, and this nation from you, your own land to live in (Genesis 12:7).
- One day I will bless people from all nations through one of your descendants (Genesis 12:3).

3. These promises were difficult for Abraham and Sarah to believe. Do you think God has given you any promises from the Bible or otherwise? Maybe you don't know. If you are aware of any promises God has given you, which ones are hardest for you to believe and why?

....
....
....
....
....
....
....
....

4. Read Jeremiah 29:11-13 (OT). What do you think are the applications of this passage to your life?

....

....

....

....

Abraham certainly had a hard time believing any of the promises God had given him because they were all contingent on him having children. Abraham and Sarah tried for years to have kids but were unsuccessful. Now that they were too old to have children, I'm sure God's promise seemed even that much more difficult to believe.

A Skeptic's View:

One of the things I have a hard time believing is this idea that God is personally involved in our lives. Even if it is true that God created the world and is in charge of it, it seems far-fetched to say that he is intimately involved in the details of each individual's life.

For example, just the other day my neighbor's daughter was involved in a terrible car accident. This is a family that is quite religious. While she is going to be okay, she has been in the hospital now for over a week. The parents talk about how grateful they are that God has spared their daughter's life. Apparently, if the car would have hit them a few more inches one way, she would have been killed instantly. Well, if God is so involved in our lives, then couldn't he have prevented the car from hitting the little girl in the first place? I just don't buy this idea that God is personally involved in my life. I am sure he has more important things to do than be concerned about someone like me.

We are told that God walks Abraham outside, shows him the stars in the sky, and says, "as you count the stars, this is how many descendants you will have" (Gen. 15:5 OT).

5. Since he and Sarah were past the age of childbearing, Abraham has a really hard time believing this could be possible. Record what Genesis 15:6 (OT) says.

....

THE FIRST EXAMPLE OF A SPIRITUAL CONVERSION

The above passage is a critical verse in the OT because it records for us the first language of "spiritual conversion." The word conversion means transformation or change. Abraham was a sinful person and did not have a right relationship with God. He was on his way toward an eternal separation from God just like everyone else who sins. God reaches down to earth, however, and chooses him out of all the people on the earth. God then gives him promises, reveals himself to him, and invites Abraham to have a personal relationship with the God of the universe. After Abraham struggles with doubt, fear, and disbelief, he finally places his faith and trust in God. As a result of this belief and faith, God "credits Abraham with righteousness" (Gen. 15:6).

What this means is that God forgives Abraham of all his sins, and gives him a new purpose for now and eternity. This change was Abraham's day of conversion. God's desire is that everyone on the earth will experience this same kind of conversion through faith, which simply means trusting God. Simply put, Abraham went from knowing about God to having a personal relationship with God from that day forward. God's plan of restoring what was lost in the Garden of Eden was now in motion.

6. Based on the example above, how would you explain spiritual conversion to someone who has never heard of this before?

GENERAL TIMELINE OF OLD TESTAMENT

Date Unknown	Creation of Heaven & Earth
2,000 BC	Abraham, Isaac, & Jacob
1,500 BC	Moses
1,450 BC	Exodus out of Egypt
1,400 BC	Promised Land entered with Joshua
1,375 BC	Period of Judges begin
1050 BC	United Kingdom begins (Saul, David, Solomon)
900 BC	Kingdom divides/splits (Israel and Judah)
700 BC	Assyria conquers northern kingdom (Israel)
600 BC	Babylon conquers Judah (city/temple destroyed, people exiled)
535 BC	Israelites return to homeland (restore God's law, temple, city)
400 BC	Close of OT revelation
0	The NT opens with John the Baptist
30 AD	Jesus' ministry, death, resurrection

HOW GOD'S PLAN UNFOLDS IN THE OLD TESTAMENT

7. The Old Testament can sometimes be intimidating and challenging to completely understand. Have you read much of the Old Testament? On a scale of 1 to 10, how much of the Old Testament storyline do you think you understand (1 - nothing, 10 - everything)?

....

If your number is low, you are not alone. Without a basic framework, it is difficult to see how all the pieces fit into the whole. If you understand what you have read in the first two chapters, and if you can follow the sequence of this next section, you will have a good handle of the Old Testament's basic progression of events. The following is a snapshot of how the Old Testament unfolds. In order for us to understand where we fit into God's plan for the world, it is important for us to know how we connect to the storyline of the Bible. Try to digest this next section as you develop a framework in your mind of the main Old Testament headlines and storyline.

To Abraham and Sarah's surprise, God fulfills his promise to them in their old age by giving them a son named Isaac. God's plan was now in motion. He was building a family on the earth that would reestablish relationship and representation. Isaac later has a son named Jacob. God has a personal encounter with Jacob, and a result, changes Jacob's name to "Israel," which means "he struggles with God" (Gen. 32:28). Jacob (Israel) had twelve sons, and these twelve sons and their extended families became known as the twelve tribes of Israel. Over the course of the next 400 years, these twelve tribes multiply to comprise over a million people and become their own people group known simply as "Israel." This was the nation God chose and created himself.

The people of Israel ended up in Egypt and are enslaved there. They cried out to God for freedom, and God freed them through many powerful miracles and the leadership of a man named Moses. God eventually brought them into the land that he promised Abraham some

600 years earlier. Two of the three promises mentioned earlier have now been fulfilled: 1) a nation has formed from Abraham, and 2) they have their own land. God is considered the king of the nation and the father of his family. However, the Israelites eventually want to be like the other nations around them, and so they tell God they want a human king. This saddens God, because he knows this won't be good for them in the long run, but he grants their request. The first king's name is Saul, the second king is David, and the third king is Solomon. David stood out, among the three, as the only one who really became a godly leader in charge of God's nation, but even he failed due to his own struggles with sin.

The fourth king, Rehoboam, failed so miserably that Israel had a civil war and split into two nations. Israel's disobedience became so bad that God's judgment ultimately fell upon them. Ungodly nations waged war against the Israelites, exiling (removing) them from their homeland for seventy years. This was a win for Satan who opposed God's people and one of the saddest days in Israel's history. God's grace was then extended again, and he allowed many of them to return to their homeland and rebuild what was destroyed due to war. However, it was never quite the same.

Although the Old Testament ends on a sour note, it offers a seed of hope for the future. The third promise to Abraham (one of his descendants would bless all nations) was not yet fulfilled, nor was God's desire for humans to express relationship and representation. The relationship between God and his people was a roller-coaster ride that saw more disappointments and failures than successes. In the end, however, God's prophets offered hope, predicting a coming king (messiah) and a day of God's judgment where his enemies will be destroyed and where his people will be fully blessed.

8. As you seek to understand how you fit into God's story, knowing that Israel had such a struggle, in what ways can you relate to the Israelites' attempt to live for God through constant setbacks and poor decisions?

....

....

....

Personal Story from Author

As I think about my wife and four kids today, my desire is that our family will do the two things God wanted Israel to do in the Old Testament: have a close and intimate relationship with him and represent him on the earth. As part of our identity with God, there are many things we do together that flow out of our relationship with him. We pray to him together; we read the Bible together, listening for his voice; we talk about God; we try to obey him; we seek forgiveness and forgive one another; we are thankful for his grace; we sing to him; we go to him when we have need, and we want to please him. God is the most important person in our family. He is at the center of our relationships.

We also try to do things as a family to represent him to others and advance his kingdom on the earth. We serve people; we pray for people who have needs; we share the gospel with people; we forgive people who hurt us; we try to take care of the environment; we pray for people to be healed of physical or spiritual problems; we try to stand up for truth against lies, and we try to show respect for authority. We still make mistakes, however, and need to work on our relationship together with God and better represent him against Satan's kingdom. Sometimes it feels like two steps forward and one step back, but I think overall we are making progress. It is encouraging to try to live for God as a family.

WHOSE KINGDOM DID YOUR FAMILY ADVANCE?

9. The following question might be a sensitive one to answer. As you think about your childhood, what was the main emphasis in your home? Were there times when the family revolved life around a relationship with God and advanced his kingdom on the earth? Or were there times when it seemed like other things became the focus in the home like money, sports, violence, fear, conflict, or simply spiritual passivity? In what ways did it seem like your family advanced God's kingdom and in what ways did it seem to advance Satan's kingdom?

10. Whether you are old enough to have your own family or not, write down a vision of your existing or future family. What do you think a family focused on God would look like in practical ways?

CHAPTER SUMMARY

Adam and Eve, as the parents of the human race, were commissioned by God to build a human family on the earth. God was to be at the center of their lives as they related to him and represented him by taking care of the creation.

After all this was destroyed through Adam and Eve's sin, Satan was building a different kind of kingdom on the earth. Spiritual conversion, which is a complete life change, would now be required to restore people to this original plan and to move them from Satan's kingdom to God's kingdom.

God chose a couple named Abraham and Sarah, led them to spiritual conversion, and commissioned them to build a new kind of family on the earth. This family became known as the nation of Israel. They were to walk with God and extend his kingdom on earth. While they had glimpses of success, they never completely fulfilled God's intention. God's desire for a family on the earth was never fully met by the Jewish people in the Old Testament. They focused too much on external behavior and didn't have enough internal change. This reality reveals that religion and outward ritual alone fail to bring us into a relationship with God. This disappointment led them to long for a deliverer, a new king who would bless them and fully restore their relationship with God as his people on the earth.

God's desire for individual families and an extended family following him is still his heartbeat today. What didn't happen in the Old Testament was about to be displayed by Jesus in the New Testament.

QUESTIONS OR JOURNAL REFLECTIONS

CHAPTER FOUR

CHAPTER FOUR

THE MODEL RELATIONSHIP: JESUS AND HIS FATHER

At twenty-one years old, I had never read the Bible. In my mind, the Bible was nothing more than one of many religious documents detailing humanity's interpretation and pursuit of God. I had a general belief in God, but it had nothing to do with anything I had read in the Bible. All of that began to change, however, during my spiritual quest in London. Although my host family was not religious, I felt drawn one day to ask them for a Bible. Perplexed by my request, they took one off their shelf, dusted it off, and gave it to me. I opened to the first book in the New Testament, The Gospel of Matthew, which is an account of Jesus' life.

As I began reading, Jesus' words and life gripped my heart and mind. Tears started rolling down my cheek as I started understanding the Bible for the first time in my life. I loved reading about sports, philosophy, and even spirituality, but nothing penetrated my heart like the Bible.

How was it that the very thing I had ridiculed for my entire life was now impacting my heart? I had so many negative assumptions about the Bible, and yet I had never read it for myself. Even though I didn't know it at the time, God was pursuing me as a loving father pursues a lost child.

WHAT YOU WILL LEARN IN THIS CHAPTER

Jesus is divine in nature, and his entrance to the earth was miraculous. He did not come to condemn people but to save them from their sinful lifestyles. He came to bring hope and the path of God's forgiveness.

Jesus not only taught what it means to have a healthy relationship with God, he modeled it. Relationship has to do with intimacy and mutual love. Jesus had an identity that was anchored in his father's love for him. Because his identity was wrapped up in his relationship with God the Father, he demonstrated this by lifestyle choices that were different than those around him. In the same way, Jesus taught that God wants to adopt us into his family and change our identity as well (John 1:12-13). God wants to become our loving Father. Jesus intentionally showed us what this looks like, and he invites us into the same kind of relationship with God.

WAITING FOR THE PROMISED MESSIAH

Although the Old Testament ends with disappointment, it promises hope. The Jewish people were anticipating and waiting for a Messiah and Savior. The Old Testament closes by saying that the Messiah will be preceded by a prophet who will announce his coming.

God's family in the Old Testament, the nation of Israel, waited on the Messiah for centuries. There is a 400 year gap between the end of the Old Testament and the opening of the New Testament. The New Testament opens with a prophet named John who tells people that the long awaited Messiah is coming soon. His predominant message was one of turning away from sin (repentance) as a way of preparing oneself to receive the Messiah (Matthew. 3:1-2). As people repented of sin, John would immerse them in water ("baptize") as a symbolic act of spiritual cleansing and a new start. Repentance is sorrow over sin and a desire to live for God. Baptism is a practice of being submerged in water as a symbol of cleansing and a new path in life. It was revealed to John that one day he would baptize the Messiah himself. Although Jesus didn't need cleansing from sin, he was baptized as an example for the rest of us to follow.

1. Read Matthew 3:13-17. As Jesus was baptized by John, record what happens:

....

....

....

....

JESUS WAS BOTH HUMAN AND DIVINE

Before looking at this close relationship Jesus and the Father had together, it is important to understand who Jesus is and where he comes from. When God introduced Jesus as his son, and himself as his Father, we also see the Holy Spirit descending from heaven in the form of a dove (Matt 3:16). Although the crowds didn't completely understand this, God was revealing himself in a threefold way (Father, Son, and Holy Spirit). God is one being, but he reveals himself to us in three "persons." This reality, known as the Trinity, is difficult for us to grasp. How God can be one, and yet three, seems like a contradiction. As noted in chapter one, however, an aspect of God's holiness is that he is beyond our ability to fully comprehend him. This is also an example when the Bible and our reason contradict each other, and we must choose which source of authority is higher.

God the Father, God the Son, and God the Holy Spirit have a perfect community. They love each other and have complete unity together. Jesus leaves the glory of heaven, comes down to earth, and becomes a human being. This is why Jesus is referred to as the God-man. He is fully God and fully human (I Tim. 2:5, John 1:1, John 8:58).

2. Read Matthew 1:18-25 (NT). Jesus was not conceived by two human parents. According to the passage, which is commonly known as the Christmas story, how was Jesus conceived?

....

....

Jesus' birth was a miraculous event. In an unprecedented way, God himself left heaven, entered into space and time, came to earth, and became a human being. While the Jewish people were waiting for the Messiah, they had no idea that this descendant of Abraham would actually be God's divine son, coming to earth as a human being.

DISCUSS IT TOGETHER

The claim that Jesus was divine led most of the Jewish people to reject him. In the Old Testament, God used many different names for himself. In Exodus 3:14, God told Moses one of his names, "I am." With your study partner reflect on the exchange Jesus has with the Jewish people found in John 8:37-59. Notice the struggle the people had believing that Jesus was truly God in human flesh. Many of us have a similar struggle believing this. Discuss the obstacles you or others might have with the claim Jesus was making.

3. When Jesus referred to himself with the title "I am," there was no doubt the Jewish people understood the significance of his statement. How do we know they understood this based on their reaction in John 8:58-59 (NT)?

....

....

....

....

JESUS IS INTRODUCED AS GOD'S SON

Now that we understand where the Bible says Jesus came from, let's go back to his baptism. John had been baptizing crowds of people to prepare them to meet and receive the long awaited Messiah. He now makes it known that the man in front of him is the one everyone has been waiting to see. After he baptizes him, a voice from the heavens says, "This is my son, whom I love; with him I am well pleased" (Matt 3:17).

The announcement from heaven was God's introduction of Jesus to the earth, and it was no accident that God used family language. God calls Jesus his son, and he says in front of everyone that he loves his son and is pleased with his son. Not only does this describe Jesus as a son, but it also describes God as a father/dad. Why did God choose to use this family kind of language? No other relationship on the earth runs deeper than the parent-child relationship; Jesus and the Father were demonstrating the kind of love relationship God desires with all his people.

4. Do you think it is possible for you to have a relationship with the God of the universe similar to the loving relationship between an earthly parent and child? Explain.

....

....
....
....
....
....

While parent-child relationships reflect the most intimate and loyal of all human relationships, the reality is that often we see struggle, tension, and conflict between parents and children.

No one had ever seen a relationship between God and a human that was free from sin and free of any influence from Satan's kingdom. When Jesus came to earth, people saw it for the first time, and they were amazed.

DISCUSS IT TOGETHER

Think about your relationship with your parents. Whether it was when you were young or the way it is now, more than likely there are both healthy and unhealthy facets to this relationship. Discuss together how this relationship (the good and the bad) might affect your ability to have a close relationship with God as a loving dad or parent today.

Personal Story from Author:

My parents divorced when I was five years old, and so I became the "man of the house" at an early age. I grew up with my mom and my sister and saw my dad every other weekend. Sometimes it was even less than that when he lived farther away. While we made the best of it, this isn't the way God intended a family to function and relate to one another. Due to this family breakup, my mom often had to take on roles of both parents (which was difficult for her), and my dad was unable to be there for me growing up as much as he would have liked (which was difficult for him).

Their divorce was difficult for both of them, and of course it was not easy for my sister and me either. It deeply affected the way we understood family relationships. Our parents still loved us, but at times it was confusing and troubling; it created in us a deep longing for a healthy family. As I think about my friends, I don't know many that actually had

> strong and healthy family relationships the way God intended (with him as the focal point). One of my friends experienced the early death of a parent. Another had parents who fought a lot. Quite a few had divorced parents, and many had parents who did not serve God together. Most people I knew had various family struggles.
>
> Broken homes and unhealthy families are even more prevalent today than they were when I was young. Today with divorce, single parent families, blended families, and everything in between, it is hard to know what God originally intended family to look like. While God does bless families no matter what they look like today, there are many ways the family is breaking down. Even though my wife and I are trying to provide a healthy and godly environment for our kids today, we know that we are making mistakes along the way as well. No wonder most of us have a hard time really understanding our relationship with God as a loving parent. On some level, we all have dysfunction in our families.

Throughout Scripture, we get a glimpse of the kind of relationship Jesus and God the Father had together. Often when we read the Bible, God speaks to our hearts in certain ways. After you read each passage, write down an observation you make on your own, or write down something from the passage that God seems to be emphasizing to you.

5. John 5:17-23 (NT)

....
....
....
....

6. John 14:2-13

....
....
....
....
....

A Skeptic's View:

One of the things I have never understood is why religion in our world produces so much hate, violence, and division. One would think that religion would lead people to more love, acceptance, and unity in our world. Whether it is religious conflict in the Middle East, Africa, Europe, Russia, or any other areas of the world, we see people going to war against other people in the name of religion.

Frankly, I don't see it much differently in our country. Christians say they have the "right way;" Jews say they are right; Muslims say they are right; Buddhists say they are right; and atheists say they are right. Everyone thinks their beliefs are true and everyone else's views are false. What is even worse is that each religion has division and conflict within itself. Within Christianity, for example, there are Baptists, Catholics, Lutherans, Presbyterians, Methodists, Episcopalians, and more, all saying they are right and the others are wrong. One of the reasons I don't want to be involved with religion is because I see what it does to so many people. Who would want to be part of this circus? Not me! I will keep serving God my own way, the way I best understand, and I will leave organized religion and all the bickering that goes on about who's right and who's wrong to others.

JESUS TEACHES A NEW WAY OF LIVING

As Jesus modeled what it meant to have a close relationship with God, he also modeled and taught its implications. God changes us from within, and then, those changes are seen in how we think and in the choices we make in life. For someone who has never read the Bible and wants to begin reading it for the first time, it is best to begin reading one of the Gospels (Matthew, Mark, Luke, and John). These are the first four books of the New Testament, and they are all accounts of the life and teachings of Jesus.

Living for God as our Father is not only about our identity in his family; it also includes a lifestyle of seeking to obey the teachings of Jesus. The following is a sampling of Jesus' teachings on what it looks like to live in God's kingdom.

LOVING OUR ENEMIES

7. Read Matthew 5:43-48 (NT). Think about some people (e.g. co-workers, family members, neighbors) who do not treat you well or whom you do not like. List some specific ways you could love them selflessly this week.

....
....
....
....

Many people hated Jesus for a variety of reasons, but he never retaliated, never mistreated them, and never returned evil for evil. We are called to follow his example, and he will empower us to do it if we step out in obedience to him.

SEXUAL PURITY

8. Read Matthew 5:27-30 (NT). Put in your own words what Jesus says about what it would look like for you to be sexually pure in your thought-life.

....
....
....
....

Jesus lived out sexual purity and taught others to do the same. What is amazing is that Jesus went well beyond the outward acts of purity. He taught people how to be pure in their thoughts. God originally created us to have an exclusive sexual relationship with our spouse. This includes not entertaining sexual thoughts with boyfriends, girlfriends, fiancés, co-workers, or anyone outside of a marriage relationship. This was a revolutionary teaching in Jesus' day (and ours!), but he not only taught it, he lived it.

NOT BEING MOTIVATED BY THE OPINIONS OF OTHERS

9. Read Matthew 6:1-4 (NT). Write down how your life or thinking would be different if you were not motivated by the opinion of others.

....

....

....

....

It is so natural for us to want people to like us. Often we try to make sure others notice our "good deeds." Jesus teaches that we should indeed do these things, but our motivation should be to please our Father in heaven, not to be praised by others.

LOVING GOD, NOT MONEY OR THINGS

10. Read Matthew 6:19-24 (NT). Think about the things in your life that are really important to you. Maybe it's your house, car, retirement account, money, clothes, electronics, sports, hobbies, or even family. God blesses his children with many things (none of which are bad in and of themselves), but he always wants to be the most important priority in our lives. As you think about your life, what do you think you are tempted to value more than God? Explain why.

....

....

....

....

COMPASSION AND LOVE FOR OTHERS

11. Read Luke 10:25-37 (NT). Quiet yourself and spend a few minutes praying that God would show you how he wants you to apply this passage to your life. Record what comes to mind and what you think God is telling you regarding Jesus' teaching here.

....
....
....
....

What is interesting about this story is that the one who didn't have compassion was the more outwardly religious person. The one who did exercise compassion, however, did so by crossing racial and cultural boundaries. Jews and Samaritans had a long history of racial tension. Not only was Jesus teaching compassion and love for others, he was also teaching the importance of crossing cultural and racial boundaries to do it. Jesus lived out and taught about racial harmony.

Becoming a part of God's family changes our lifestyle and character. As Jesus taught all these principles of life, he was teaching people how to live out their identity as God's sons and daughters.

GOD WANTS TO ADOPT YOU INTO HIS FAMILY

Most of us already think that we are God's children simply because he is our creator. While it is true that God created every individual on the earth, God personally adopts those who place faith in Jesus.

As we saw in the last chapter, God selected Abraham and Sarah to relate to him and represent him, and he began building a family from their physical descendants. Today, God is building a spiritual family through his son, Jesus. God's family now consists of everyone on the earth who believes and follows Jesus. This reality is the fulfillment of the third promise given to Abraham back in the early pages of Genesis: "One of your descendants will one day bless all nations" (Genesis 12:3).

12. Read Romans 8:15-17 (NT). What does this passage mean regarding the truth that God wants to adopt you into his family as a loving parent?

....
....
....

GOD WANTS TO GIVE YOU A NEW IDENTITY

We saw in Chapter Two of this study that we started sinning against God very early in life. God's desire, however, is that your identity will no longer be focused on the sins you have committed. God wants to give you a new identity as his child; a relationship like the one Jesus has with God the Father.

13. Do you think you could ever see yourself as a child of God, someone that God is proud of and loves unconditionally? Do you think your self identity could change so much that you no longer felt like you constantly disappoint God or that you had to earn his love? Explain your answer.

....
....
....
....
....
....

GOD IS READY TO WELCOME YOU HOME WITH OPEN ARMS

God knows we have messed up our lives, but he is forgiving and welcomes us back with open arms. One of the most powerful pictures of this reality is a story Jesus told to a group of religious teachers. As you read this story, ask God to speak to your heart, and be open to whatever aspect of the story he wants to apply to your life.

14. Take your time and read Luke 15:11-32. Write out some observations you think best apply to you and your life.

....
....
....
....

CHAPTER SUMMARY

The Old Testament closed with disappointment. The New Testament, however, opens with an introduction to the greatest intervention of God in the history of the universe. God's son comes down from heaven to earth, becomes a human being, and shows the world what it means to be in God's family. Jesus shows everyone what a close relationship with God looks like. This was the first time anyone had ever witnessed what God originally desired for humanity. It was almost like the Garden of Eden revisited.

With great love and pride, God introduces his son, Jesus, to the world. This was Jesus' identity. Through Jesus, God wants to give us this same identity today: beloved children of whom God is proud. God is ready to welcome us into his loving family!

QUESTIONS OR JOURNAL REFLECTIONS

CHAPTER FIVE

THE CALL TO GIVE UP EVERYTHING AND FOLLOW JESUS

During that evening in London when I started to read the book of Matthew, I have to admit that I had no idea that God was adopting me into his family and was ready to change my life. Although I didn't think of myself as a Christian at the time, I did believe in God, and I knew I was on a spiritual journey. That night, however, something changed. This something would only be realized later when I looked back. My host family thought it was honorable and refreshing to see a young college kid reading an ancient, religious book like the Bible and discussing it with them on occasion, but even I was unsure whether this was simply a phase or something more permanent.

One of my best friends from high school came over to England after the semester ended, and we hitchhiked and backpacked around England, Wales, and Scotland. One day we got picked up by an older gentleman in a very small car. My friend and I scrunched in, and one of his first questions was, "Are you both believers?" I felt like we were in some kind of British television comedy. My friend and I kind of looked at each other, were shocked by the question, and had no idea what to say. I felt like I was becoming one of these "believers," but it was all still very new and at times confusing for me. My friend and I simply shrugged our shoulders and said, "We don't know."

Some people can specify the exact moment of their conversion to Jesus because they experienced a sudden, radical transformation. When I reflect back, I would say my "moment" was that evening when I first opened the book of Matthew. That was the moment my heart began to change. I realize now that my answer to the man in the car should have been, "Yes," but I really didn't understand the full extent of what was happening to me spiritually until later. My life was on the brink of significant changes.

WHAT YOU WILL LEARN IN THIS CHAPTER

Jesus modeled what it looked like to be a child of God. At the same time, however, he made it possible for everyone else to have this kind of relationship with God by going to the cross and willingly laying down his life. On the cross, Jesus received the punishment that sinful people like us deserved. This made a way for us to find forgiveness for our sins and a relationship with God.

The way we receive this forgiveness from God is by repenting of our sins and putting our trust in Jesus. In this chapter we will do some self-reflection and come to terms with where we are in our journey with God. People cannot move forward in their spiritual life until they understand where they stand with God presently.

JESUS GOES TO THE CROSS

God's plan from the beginning was that his Son would come to the earth, live a perfect life, die in our place, and be raised from the dead in victory. The night before Jesus' crucifixion, Jesus had a meal with his twelve disciples and tells them what is about to happen. This meal is still celebrated today and is commonly called the Lord's Supper, communion, or the Eucharist (from a Greek word meaning "thanksgiving"). Our relationship with God is centered on what happened when Jesus died for our sins. This is why the church participates in the practice of communion today. Since our relationship with God depends on Jesus' death on the cross, this consistent practice of communion is a reminder of what Jesus has done for us.

JESUS' MESSAGE: A LIFE CHANGE TOWARD GOD

Jesus talked about the way people could be adopted into God's family. He said one needs to have a change of heart (repent) and trust him for everything (faith). At the foundation of this trust is a belief in the gospel message that Jesus died, was buried, and rose on the third day (I Cor. 15:1-4). These two principles of repentance and belief (or faith) become the means by which anyone can be forgiven by God and begin to live life in God's kingdom now (Acts 20:21). It is the way to begin a relationship with God in this life and ultimately receive the gift of living with God forever.

WHAT IS REPENTANCE?

If repentance is necessary to receive forgiveness and adoption into God's family, we must make sure we understand it clearly. Let's take the example of someone lying on his time card in order to get paid more for his job. If the person gets caught, and he begins to break down crying in front of his boss because he is so ashamed, he is experiencing sorrow and shame for getting caught. He may even admit that he had been lying, which would be confession. Confession and sorrow, however, are only part of repentance (2 Cor. 7:10-11). Confession on its own is inadequate. Repentance signifies a "turning" has taken place in his heart. Repentance means the person is sorrowful and saddened because he knows his lying was wrong before God, and now his desire is to stop lying and live in the truth. Repentance is a heart change that desires to avoid sin. It is a turn away from sin and a desire to live for God.

1. What does Jesus say will happen to people who do not repent of their sins in life according to Luke 13:3 (NT)? What do you think this means?

....

....

....

....

Jesus spoke with many people who thought they were God's children because they were born into the right family, participated in the right religious activities, or avoided the wrong activities. When Jesus interacted with them, however, he found their lifestyles were no different from other people in the world. They were simply "acting the part" and had not been changed from the inside. This is why Jesus called them "hypocrites," which was an old word that meant "actor."

2. What do you think Jesus meant in Matthew 23:25-28 (NT)?

....

....

....

....

The problem many people had in Jesus' day is the same problem many have today. They have tried to focus on external behavior change without ever experiencing the inner change of repentance. This causes many people to think they are "Christians" because they were born in a religious home, go to church, or try to be good citizens and neighbors. The problem is that many have not yet been adopted into God's family. It is like trying to grow before being born.

The religious leaders became very confused with Jesus' teaching, and many of them became downright angry. They did not like the fact that he was challenging their claims on God. Jesus continued to talk to people about the inward change of the heart (repentance), which will then naturally lead to outward changes in behavior and lifestyle (faith). Jesus was describing how to live from the inside-out.

3. Read Luke 18:10-14 (NT). What do you think Jesus is saying is most important?

....

....

....

Once we repent in our heart, the natural result of that repentance is changed behavior and lifestyle. Sometimes, aspects of this change are seen overnight, but most of the time, the change is gradual. If repentance in the heart has taken hold, though, outward change will eventually come. If we don't see this outward change over time, we have cause to be concerned. Copy the following verses that teach the principle of inner repentance verified by life change:

4. Matthew 3:8

....

....

5. Acts 26:20 (NT) (second half of verse)

....

....

6. James 2:17

....

....

....

7. What do you think I John 2:3-6 is teaching?

....

....

....

....

....

The evidence of our inward repentance is our changed lifestyle. While no one is perfect, and we will always battle with sin, those who have been forgiven by God and adopted into his family will choose to live differently than those who don't know God. Followers of Jesus really do follow Jesus. This means we obey his commands and model our life on his. God grants us a great deal of grace in this process because we often take two steps forward and one step back. It is not a life of perfection, but rather a life of humility, dependence on God, and gradual progress in kingdom living.

JESUS BECOMES OUR SUBSTITUTE

When we repent of our sin and place faith in Jesus, something spiritual and miraculous happens to us; God does something that no one can fully explain. God takes all of our sinful thoughts, words, actions, past, present, and future sins and transfers them to Jesus, who took the punishment for them on the cross. We are then free from the punishment we deserve, and our relationship with God is restored. In this way, Jesus becomes our representative. The greatest display of God's holiness and God's love is at the cross.

8. Read Mark 14:35-36 (NT). In this passage, Jesus is nearing his death on the cross, and he knows he is about to experience punishment on behalf of the sins of the world (including yours). Jesus is in a real battle in this moment, and the Bible says "his sweat was like drops of blood falling to the ground" (Luke 22:44). He was willing to do this because of his love for his Father and all those he was dying for (including you). How do you think Jesus' death on the cross demonstrates both God's holiness and God's love?

....

....

....

....

....

Without repentance and faith in Jesus, the Bible tells us that relationship with God is impossible. There is no other way to remove your sin. You cannot transform your life or stop sinning by yourself, nor can you do anything to take away the penalty of your past sins. There are only two possible ways to take care of your sin: Either you try to take care of it yourself and experience a permanent separation from God in hell, or you can let Jesus take care of it, allowing him to be your substitute, paying the penalty for your sin himself. It is a decision only you can make. This offer of salvation and forgiveness in Christ is called the gospel, which is an old word that means "good news." Faith in Jesus is the only way we can be adopted into God's family and the only way our relationship with God as our Father/Dad can be restored.

A Skeptic's View:

The Bible is a good storybook, and it certainly makes for an intriguing storyline that a divine being came down from heaven, became a human being, showed us how to live, and then died in our place. It makes for a good novel, but once you start talking about centering your entire life around a story that no one can prove is correct, things get a little wacky. Who is willing to have that kind of blind faith? Certainly not me! Can anyone prove that Jesus walked the earth? Can anyone prove that Jesus was God in the flesh? Can anyone prove that his death had any meaningful bearing to the history of the world? Can anyone prove the Bible is not just human interpretation of a legend or a handed-down story? Can anyone prove there is life after death? The answer to all these questions is a resounding No. And yet, millions of people have devoted their entire lives to Jesus and his teachings. If doing this makes them happy or helps them make a greater contribution to society, then I think there is merit in that. Let's not pretend, however, that anyone has any proof that any of this stuff is true. In the same way, no one can prove any of the other major religions of the world are true or false either. I am glad people are sincere and have convictions about their beliefs, but in the end, everyone's faith (or lack thereof) is just a stab in the dark. Don't blame me for not wanting to waste my time on this.

FAITH ISN'T BLIND BUT REASONABLE

The Bible is one of the most well-documented pieces of literature in the history of the world. There is strong manuscript evidence for the historical reliability of the New Testament, and there are countless archeological findings that historically support many of the biblical accounts. Nowhere does the Bible try to prove God exists, however. The Bible simply says that God has created the world and humans in such a way that we instinctively know there is a creator (Rom. 2:15). And if there is a personal creator, it would make sense that he would intentionally reveal himself to the people he created rather than be uninvolved. These things make rational sense. Think of how much more "faith" it would take to believe all we see in this world came here by chance due to a random explosion billions of years ago.

9. Read Acts 17:1-34. Here we see one of Jesus' leaders communicating the gospel to people who had no Bible background. As you read this,

what strikes you about the approach Paul takes as he engages these unbelievers?

....
....
....
....
....

THE BIBLE IS GOD'S LETTER TO THE WORLD

As we consider repenting and placing faith in Jesus, it is important to realize that the biblical account of Jesus' life and teaching is reliable and God-inspired.

10. Read 2 Timothy 3:16-17 (NT) and write down what you think it means.

....
....
....
....
....
....
....

The Bible is not the human interpretation of God; it is God's revelation of himself. Although God can speak to us in many ways — dreams, visions, impressions, circumstances, conversations with other people — the Bible remains the anchor of God's truth. Everything must align with the truth of God's word. Although God used human beings to record his words, we can trust that the words within the Bible are true. It is written by many different authors, across many different continents, and over a period of more than 1500 years. And yet the Bible contains no errors, no contradictions, and communicates a unified message of God's saving activity. While we do not worship the Bible, we ought to honor it as God's authoritative message to us (2 Tim. 3:16-17). It is like a love letter from God to his children, an invitation to step into God's kingdom as members of his family.

Personal Story from Author:

Growing up, our family went to church mainly on holidays. I believed in God but had never repented and put my faith in Jesus. Therefore, I did not have a living relationship with God, nor had I been forgiven of my sins. When I was twelve years old or so, I went to a summer Bible camp at a church, and one of the teachers asked, "Who here would like to be forgiven of all the wrong things they have done, and who would like to go to heaven when they die?" Well, what kid would say no to that? So I raised my hand just like many others did. The teacher then said, "For those of you who raised your hands, repeat this prayer after me, 'I confess to God that I am a sinner, and I believe Jesus died for my sins…" After the prayer she said, "Whoever prayed this prayer has just become a Christian, and when you die, you will be with God in heaven forever and ever."

The following years after that event, my life never changed, and I never tried to follow Jesus or his teachings. I was a relatively good person, but I did not center my life around living for Jesus. In high school, I eventually started to live an even deeper sinful lifestyle. This continued during my early college years, and if you would have asked me if I had a relationship with God, I would have said yes because I simply believed he existed. The reality, however, is that I was as spiritually lost as anyone ever has been. I just didn't know it.

THERE IS NO MAGICAL PRAYER TO RECEIVE FORGIVENESS

There is not a set prayer or pattern in the Bible that outlines a single way people came to faith in Christ. It happened in many different ways. Read each of these three passages and record how repentance and faith looked differently in each passage.

11. Luke 5:17-20 (NT)

....

....

....

12. Luke 7:36-50 (NT)

....

....

13. Acts 16:22-34 (NT)

....

....

....

....

HOW DO I KNOW IF I REALLY AM FORGIVEN AND A FOLLOWER OF JESUS?

Many people believe they are Christians because they believe God exists, or they go to church, or think Jesus was a pretty cool guy. An inner conversion of the heart through repentance and faith, however, is the only way God forgives us and adopts us into his family.

14. Read Matthew 7:17-23 (NT). Jesus is addressing the danger of self-deception. What a tragedy some could face at the end of life. Although it is not an easy question, do you think you could be deceived about where you are spiritually, or do you feel confident that know where you are at based on what the Bible teaches?

....

....

....

....

....

15. What responsibility do all of us have according to 2 Corinthians 13:5?

....

....

....

Below is a tool to help in our evaluation process. On this diagram place a "B" next to the number you feel you were before starting this book. Next, write a "T" where you think you are spiritually today.

YOUR FAITH JOURNEY

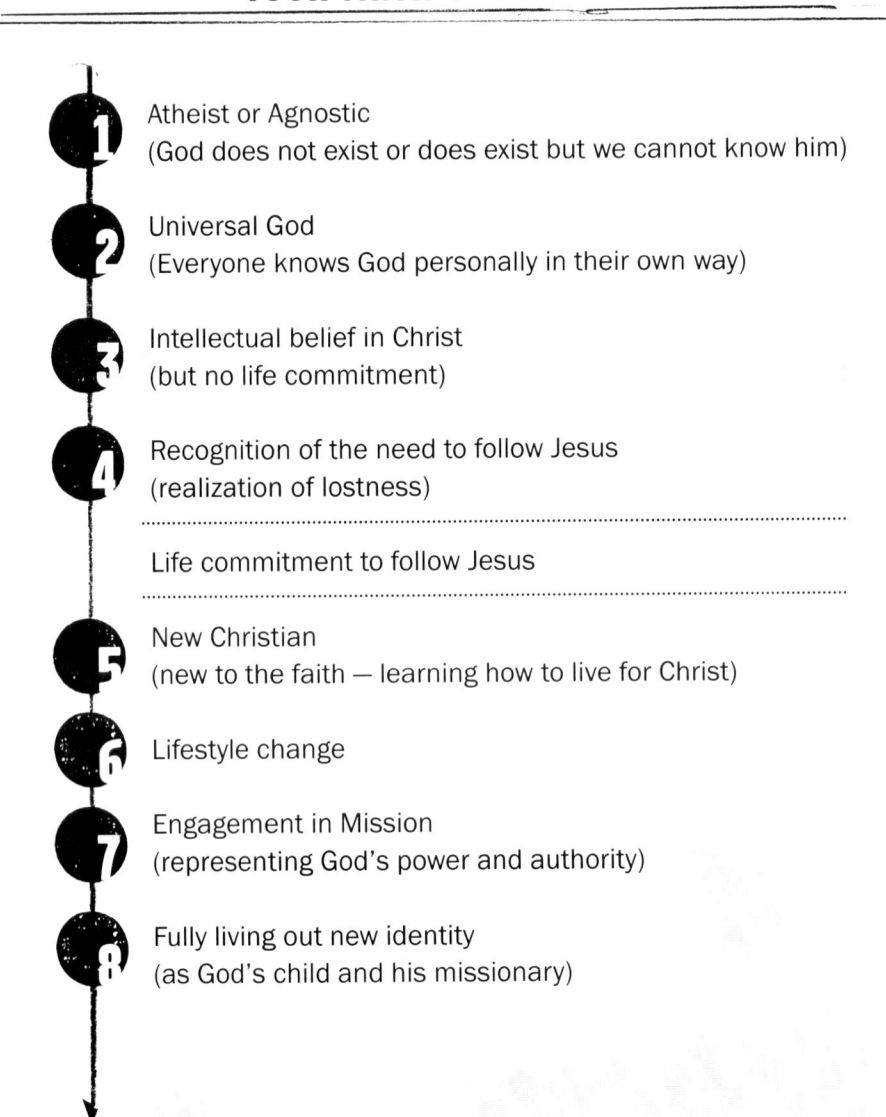

1 Atheist or Agnostic
(God does not exist or does exist but we cannot know him)

2 Universal God
(Everyone knows God personally in their own way)

3 Intellectual belief in Christ
(but no life commitment)

4 Recognition of the need to follow Jesus
(realization of lostness)

....
Life commitment to follow Jesus
....

5 New Christian
(new to the faith — learning how to live for Christ)

6 Lifestyle change

7 Engagement in Mission
(representing God's power and authority)

8 Fully living out new identity
(as God's child and his missionary)

16. If you placed your "T" before the step of "life commitment," which means you have not yet repented and surrendered your life to Jesus in faith, are you willing to make that decision today, and if not, what would prevent you?

....
....
....
....
....

CHAPTER SUMMARY

Jesus died in our place and then three days later rose from the dead. Believing in God, trying to be a good person, and serving in a church are all good things but not the ultimate indicators of someone who has been adopted into God's family and forgiven of their sins. Repentance (an inward heart change) and faith in Jesus are the two things God requires. This inward conversion will lead to a changed life. Jesus says "If you love me, you will obey my teachings" (John 14:23). It is important that every person engage in some self-reflection on their spiritual journey in life because most people who are spiritually lost do not know it. It is only when we understand the gospel and Jesus' words on repentance and faith that we can accurately evaluate our lives. God's offer of forgiveness and adoption into his family is given to anyone who is willing to repent, believe, and follow Jesus. No matter what we have done, we are never beyond God's ability to forgive us and give us a new life in his kingdom.

QUESTIONS OR JOURNAL REFLECTIONS

....
....
....
....

CHAPTER SIX

THE MISSION OF BRINGING HEAVEN TO EARTH

After my two semesters in England, because of the spiritual transformation that had taken place, I flew back home a different person than when I left. I was now ready to follow Jesus and knew one of the things that meant was to find others who were doing that too. It was time to do something that would have been unthinkable for me only six months earlier - start looking for a church. Since I had no church background, the possibilities were wide open. Ann Arbor, Michigan, wasn't exactly known for its churches, but then again, I really didn't know what I was looking for in a church.

I was still skeptical of organized religion, and at the time, I didn't know much about the Bible. However, I did want to find a community of like-minded people who wanted to pursue this "Jesus thing" like I did. I decided to try every church I could: Methodist, Catholic, Presbyterian, Baptist, Lutheran, Independent, etc. I got a lot of strange stares in many of the churches as I walked in with my Bible in hand. It took me quite a few months, but eventually I landed in a community where I felt both welcomed and challenged. God led me to a family of believers who invested in me and my growth as a follower of Jesus.

For some reason, I knew enough about following Jesus to realize that it should be done in community with others. Once I dove into community life with other believers, my spiritual life really took off.

WHAT YOU WILL LEARN IN THIS CHAPTER

Living out a life in God's kingdom entails helping others restore their relationship with God and reverse the effects of sin. Sin and Satan's kingdom were absent when God first created Adam and Eve, and they will be absent when God fully restores creation in the new heaven and earth at the end of time. When Jesus left the earth after his death and resurrection, he handed off his mission to his disciples and, ultimately, to all who place their faith in him. When we believe in Jesus, the Holy Spirit enters our lives to live within us and empower us to live for Jesus and bring the future realities of heaven to the earth today. As we work together with other believers, we experience the power of God in every area of life.

JESUS GIVES HIS FINAL INSTRUCTIONS BEFORE LEAVING THE EARTH

After Jesus died on the cross and paid the penalty for sin on our behalf, God raised him from the dead three days later. Good Friday is a day when we remember God's love for the world as Jesus took our place and paid for our sin. Easter Sunday is a day we celebrate an empty tomb signifying God's power and victory over sin and its consequences. After his resurrection from the dead, Jesus appeared to his disciples over a period of forty days, giving them final instructions on how to live and carry on the mission of God's kingdom that he started and modeled for them (Acts 1:3).

OUR MISSION – HELP OTHERS RESTORE THEIR RELATIONSHIP WITH GOD

1. Read Matthew 28:16-20 (NT). This is one of Jesus' final instructions to his disciples before he leaves the earth. Just as he has been helping people restore their relationship with God by challenging them to repent and follow him, he now commissions his disciples to do the same after he is gone. As representatives of God in this world, we are entrusted with the responsibility of helping those around us restore their broken relationship with God. He also empowers us for this work through the presence and gifts of the Holy Spirit. As you read this passage, are you willing to accept this mission God has given you? Explain what you think this means in everyday life.

....

....

....
....
....
....

This idea that God wants to use us to help people find God and begin a relationship with him is something Jesus communicated to his disciples when he first called them to follow him.

2. What do you think Jesus meant in Mark 1:17 (NT)?

....
....
....
....

3. Read 2 Cor. 5:17-20 (NT) and explain how you think this passage applies to you.

....
....
....
....
....
....
....

4. How can you help your family members, friends, co-workers, and neighbors restore their relationship with God? If God desires a relationship with them, and yet their sin breaks that relationship, how can you help them receive forgiveness and begin living for God as an adopted son or daughter? If helping people repent and believe is the mission

Jesus modeled and then gave to us, how you can live this out right now with those around you? Be specific.

....
....
....
....
....
....

OUR MISSION — REVERSE THE EFFECTS OF SIN

Jesus represented God while living on the earth by reversing the effects of sin and Satan's kingdom in all areas of life, both spiritual and physical. He resolved conflict, removed pain, brought joy where there was sadness, healed disease, and even reversed death on several occasions.

5. Record Mark 6:12-13 (NT)

....
....
....
....

Notice how the disciples lived out a holistic mission in the same way Jesus did, comprising both spiritual and physical needs. Jesus wants you to help people restore their relationship with God, and he also wants you to help people physically and emotionally.

6. As you are attempting to help people repent and believe in Jesus for their spiritual restoration, how can you also help restore them in the physical arena? As you think about what life was like in the Garden of Eden, how can God use you to help bring that about in the lives of those around you? Give some practical suggestions regarding your friends, co-workers, and family members.

....

....

....

....

....

PARADISE WILL ONCE AGAIN RETURN ON A NEW EARTH

7. Read Revelation 21:1-8. Compare what you read here to what paradise looked like for Adam and Eve in the Garden of Eden before Satan and sin entered the world. Feel free to go back and skim through Chapter One to refresh your memory. Write down the similarities you see between the Garden of Eden and the new earth.

....

....

....

....

....

....

....

....

Jesus will come to the earth a second time to complete the mission he started during his first coming, and he will bring the full expression of the kingdom of God. There is coming a day when this world will end and pass away, and God will renew all things. A new earth and a new heaven will be established. Every follower of Christ will be a permanent resident in this new creation, and every unbeliever, including Satan and his demons, will be shut out of God's presence forever (Rev. 20:10-14).

Even when people are healed physically and spiritually in this life, the effects of sin still are not completely removed. People restored to God still sin, and people who get healed eventually get sick again and die. It is important to remember that the kingdom will only be partially fulfilled until Jesus returns a second time to bring complete fulfillment. This is when all the effects of sin and Satan's kingdom will be removed completely, forever. Until then, we see glimpses of God's kingdom on earth.

What we see is that the Garden of Eden in Genesis and the new earth in Revelation are the bookends, not only of the Bible, but also of the history of the universe. Right now, we are living in between these two perfect realities. Sin is rampant, and Satan's kingdom is the dominant kingdom in the world today. In the midst of this chaotic world, however, God is building his family and kingdom.

While it's true that one day God's original desire for the world will be restored to his original intention, God desires his family to advance this plan today by pushing back Satan's kingdom until Jesus returns. We are to bring these glimpses of God's glory by living out his kingdom now.

BRINGING HEAVEN TO EARTH BY THE POWER OF THE SPIRIT

Notice how the following traits WERE true in the Garden of Eden in the past and WILL BE true on the new earth in the future.

NO JEALOUSY	SELFLESSNESS
NO IMMORTALITY	HONESTY
NO RAGE	PERFECT HEALTH
NO HATRED	NO DISEASE
NO CONFLICT	NO DEATH
NO DYING	NO SATAN
COMPASSION	NO SIN
LOVE	REILATIONSHIP WITH GOD

We saw what paradise looked like before sin entered the world, and we see that paradise awaits our future in the new heaven and new earth.

8. Read Matthew 6:9-13 (NT). This is commonly referred to as the Lord's Prayer. Notice the instructions Jesus gives about prayer within the first two verses:
   1) Address God as Father or Dad – our identity is that we are God's children.
   2) Remember his name is holy – he is both loving AND holy.
   3) Pray for his kingdom to come to earth just like it is in heaven.

We have a glimpse of what heaven is like based on what we read in Revelation 21. God has given us a mission of bringing heaven to earth today. Knowing this restoration of God's original intention for his people is both spiritual and physical, what parts of this job excite you? What parts make you nervous or unsure?

....
....
....
....
....

Before leaving the earth, Jesus told his disciples they would receive the Holy Spirit, who would give them the ability to do what God was calling them to do. The Holy Spirit is the third person of the Trinity as mentioned in Chapter Four. God the Father is the one who has adopted us into his family; God the Son is the one who died in our place so that we can be forgiven; and God the Spirit is the one who empowers us to live out Christlike character and engage in his mission of bringing heaven to earth.

9. Read Acts 1:8 (NT). In your own words, what do you think Jesus meant by this verse?

....
....
....
....

DISCUSS IT TOGETHER

What do you think it means to fulfill the mission of bringing heaven to earth (both physically and spiritually) by the power of the Holy Spirit and not simply by our own human abilities? Discuss with your study partner.

LIVING OUT THE MISSION BASED ON OUR NEW IDENTITY IN CHRIST

Being a follower of Christ means we desire to live for him and help bring his kingdom to the earth today. We must do these things from the foundation of our new identity in Christ and the power of the Spirit.

If you have repented of your sins and placed your faith in Jesus, God has done things in your life that you cannot see. You have been forgiven of all your past, present, and future sins. You have been adopted into God's family and have become a cherished son or daughter whom he loves unconditionally. You have also received the promise of eternal life and have been given a mission right now to represent your heavenly Father. You are not the same person you used to be. You are a new person with a new identity (2 Cor. 5:17).

10. Read Psalm 103:11-13 (OT) and Romans 8:28-39 (NT). Record some of your own observations as you think about how these verses apply to you.

....
....
....
....
....

It is important for us to understand that while followers of Jesus still sin and have struggles at times, God will not punish us for our sin because Jesus was punished in our place. Romans 8:1 says, "Therefore, there is now no condemnation for those who are in Christ Jesus." We cannot earn God's love and acceptance. He gives it to us as a free gift of grace. We are always completely forgiven even if we don't feel forgiven, and we have an identity in God's family forever. As 2 Corinthians 5:17 says, "We are a new creation in Christ."

DISCUSS IT TOGETHER

Discuss with your study partner the struggles we have in really understanding our identity in Christ. Do we walk around with the constant sense that God loves us, that he is proud of us, and that he is pleased with us? Do we live like we have been given a gift, or do we keep trying to earn God's love and acceptance by our behavior?

JESUS HANDS OFF THE BATON TO THE EARLY CHURCH

Jesus only spent about three years with his disciples. When he left, he gave them the responsibility to continue what he started. As we read the account of the early Christian community (the Acts of the Apostles in the New Testament), we see imperfect disciples living out these teachings and actually doing the very things they saw Jesus doing. The early church picked up right where Jesus left off. They had a secure identity in Christ that gave them both humility and boldness. They actually believed they could do the same things Jesus did. This is what Jesus taught them when he said, "I tell you the truth, anyone who has faith in me will do what I have been doing. He will do even greater things than these, because I am going to the Father" (John 14:12).

As we read through Acts and the other books of the New Testament, we get a glimpse of how the disciples carried out Jesus' mission through the power of the Holy Spirit. The mission was expanding, and God was using imperfect people to do it. People were being restored to relationship with God and being adopted into his family.

A Skeptic's View:

The stories in the Bible are inspiring, powerful, and amazing: God parting the Red Sea, lame people walking, the blind receiving sight, nations repenting of sin, a prostitute being transformed, etc. I think people can make changes in their lives, but we certainly do not see the kinds of things the Bible describes in our everyday lives today. I know I have never seen any of these miraculous experiences. I think they are great stories, but I think they are simply legends. The stories might be beneficial if they help people believe in a God who is powerful and loving, but let's be honest: these kinds of things don't happen today.

Personal Story from Author:

I have a real desire to live like Jesus lived. I know I will make a lot of mistakes along the way, but I know that God has given me the power by his Spirit to be Christlike in my character and to engage in Jesus' mission on the earth in the same way he did. My job is to be open to him and dependent on his Spirit, and then allow him to work in me and through me to help others. This requires a willingness to step out in faith, even when it is uncomfortable. The only reason I came to Christ is because others loved me enough to pray for me and share the gospel with me – even though I rejected it many times before finally repenting and believing.

I still worry sometimes about what others think of me. For example, I know that part of engaging in Jesus' mission is to help others repent of sin and place faith in Jesus. I am in regular contact with many people who need God's forgiveness, but often I am not as bold as I should be. I try to love them and serve them, but there also comes a point when I need to share the message of the kingdom and how it applies to them. I am currently praying that my identity as God's son, whom God loves and is proud of, will lead me to better represent him and his love. I want to give away to others what I have received from God as I try to bring heaven to earth.

11. Spend a few moments in prayer and ask God to place a few people on your heart that you would love to see repent, come into God's family, and begin living out the mission of Jesus. Write down the names of the people God has laid on your heart.

....
....
....
....

DISCUSS IT TOGETHER

Talk to your study partner about the possibility of asking the people you listed to go through this Bible study with you. Even if you feel inadequate to lead, God will give you the power and the confidence to do it. You don't have to be a scholar to facilitate this kind of study. Plus, the Holy Spirit lives in you and will help you do it!

WHAT IS THE CHURCH?

Even though many people refer to certain buildings as "churches," from a biblical perspective, the church is not a building. A church is a community of believers in Jesus who love God together, love one another, and engage in his mission of bringing heaven to earth. Being part of a church is not simply about attending services on Sunday. Involvement in a church is about gathering God's family together and being part of a movement built around relationship and representation, identity in Christ, and responsibility to carry out his mission. It is a family who knows their identity and is called to action.

12. Read Acts 2:42-47. According to the last verse, what was the end result of God's people devoted to a community called God's church?

....

....

....

....

....

CHAPTER SUMMARY

Not only did Jesus show us how to engage in God's mission to the world, he gave us the power to do it through the Holy Spirit. When we are adopted into his family through repentance and faith, we gain a new identity in Christ. This identity leads us to the responsibility of representing him and advancing his mission in the world. This mission is to help others be restored to a relationship with God and to reverse the effects of sin.

There is coming a day when this world as we know it will pass away, and God will establish a new heaven and new earth. At this time, God will completely and fully reverse the effects of sin. God's original plan for creation will be restored, and all of God's children will rejoice in their new home.

In the meantime, however, Satan's kingdom is still present. We are called to consider the reality of what heaven is like and then attempt to bring the future realities of heaven to the earth by the power of the Spirit. Living for Christ and engaging in his mission is not an easy life to lead. We battle against our own sin and an enemy who works against us. It requires sacrifice, a willingness to be uncomfortable, and a daily surrender to God. However, it is the greatest life we could ever pursue.

According to the Bible, this is what God is doing in the world. His loving invitation to you is to be part of this story so that you can take your place in the story of restoration. Will you seek him? Will you follow him? Will you carry on the mission until Jesus returns or you no longer have breath? What are some ways God's Spirit is speaking to you now as you have been engaging in this study? Spend some time in reflection, and tell someone else how God is working in your life.

"You will seek me and find me when you seek me with all your heart" (Jeremiah 29:13).

QUESTIONS OR JOURNAL REFLECTIONS

CHAPTER SIX

CHAPTER SEVEN

A NEW PATH TO LIFE

As a new follower of Christ, everything seemed so different. I had a different direction in life, a desire to be a different person, and lifestyle changes started to become evident. Normally, college is thought of as a time to let loose and do things you couldn't do before, so some of my friends started to wonder why I was acting so differently. At the time, I was waiting tables and bartending on the side at a Mexican restaurant. One night after the restaurant had closed, I was talking to the chef about Jesus. My friend walked by and gave me a strange look, as if to say, "Who have you become, and what are you doing?" It was funny because after he walked by with that look, I thought to myself, "Who have I become, and what am I doing?" This was exactly what I used to hate about Christians--always trying to convert people to "their beliefs". My heart was genuine, however, and I was just trying to bring love to those around me.

I got involved in a college ministry on campus, and I got involved in a church. I hung out with people my own age, but I also hung out with young families and even older people. I started to feel a sense of "family" with others who were passionate about living for Jesus.

I started reading the Bible whenever I could. I even had the Bible on audio and would listen to it every day in between classes. It became difficult for me to study for classes because all I wanted to do was read Scripture and hang out with others who were spiritually further down the road than I was. I was like a sponge, soaking it all up; I loved growing. This affected me in many different areas of life. One example, out of many, was the area of dating.

I came to realize I had no idea how to date girls in a way that was honoring to God. Therefore, I decided to stop dating altogether until I understood purity and the purpose of dating. This shocked a lot of people and caused them to think something was wrong with me.

While many people thought I was getting too extreme with my lifestyle changes, I had several mature believers who supported me and encouraged me. I am not sure where I would be today without the support structure of fellow Jesus-followers. The need for this kind of community doesn't go away, either. Even today, many years removed from college and my initial Christian experience, I still need believers around me to encourage me, challenge me, support me, and live out the mission of God's kingdom with me together. Following Jesus was never meant to be done alone.

WHAT YOU WILL LEARN IN THIS CHAPTER

The first six chapters of this book take you on a journey of understanding the big picture of what God is doing in the world, and why God calls everyone to repent of sin and trust Jesus with their lives. This decision, along with understanding how you fit into God's overall plan for the world, is the foundation of your life in Christ.

God continues to build a family and establish a movement of his Spirit on the earth. Being a part of this movement means we live this new kind of life together in community with others. It is critical to find others who are also on this same journey. Some of the "first steps" for new followers of Jesus revolve around the following themes:
- Becoming a person who knows the Bible and the voice of the Holy Spirit
- Distinguishing between identity and activity
- Having both a mentor and "mentee" in your life
- Becoming a part of a church community on mission

THE BIBLE IS YOUR ANCHOR OF TRUTH

Chapter One discussed four sources of authority: the Bible, reason, experience, and tradition. We use these to form our beliefs about the world, but Christians hold one in highest esteem. Although God uses all of them, there is only one source that has not been affected by sin, and that is the Bible.

1. Read John 18:37-38. What does Pilate ask Jesus?

....

2. Read John 8:31-32. What does Jesus equate as truth?

....

All throughout Jesus' ministry, he addresses the need to know the truth. In John 14:6, Jesus says that he himself is the truth. Jesus equates his teaching and all of Scripture as God's truth. Through reading the Scriptures, we come to know Jesus more fully.

3. Copy Psalm 119:105.

....

....

....

4. Copy Psalm 119:11.

....

....

....

Growing in our understanding and obedience to the Scriptures is a lifelong process that will involve reading, meditating, memorizing, studying, receiving teaching, and conforming our thinking to God's truth. Followers of Jesus are marked by a rhythm of attending to the Word of God through the words of the Bible. The Bible says the Word of God is living and active (Hebrews 4:12), it changes you (I Thessalonians 2:13), it lives in you (I John 2:14), it is flawless (Proverbs 30:5), and everything it says will eventually come to pass just as it is written (Jeremiah 1:12).

Sometimes the Bible will challenge human reason, tradition, and experience. When these kinds of conflicts come up, the Bible needs to be the foundation of what we believe and practice. God communicates truth to us in many ways, but the Bible is the one authoritative source under which all other sources must be evaluated.

However, reading and studying the Bible should never be our ultimate goal. It is more like a means to an end. The point of reading the Bible is to know God and live for him. The Bible reveals who God is. It's easy for Christians to trick themselves into thinking that if they are pursuing Bible knowledge they must be growing spiritually. Jesus challenged this kind of thinking, however, when he said to the Pharisees, "You diligently study the Scriptures because you think that by them you possess eternal life. These are the Scriptures that testify about me, yet you refuse to come to me to have life" (John 5:39-40). We read and study the Bible so that we can have his word flow through us as we live for him. Knowing or living for God is the "end," and the Bible is the primary "means" to get there.

5. If the Bible is so important in our journey of knowing and living for God, what kind of rhythm have you or should you establish to read, study, memorize, and meditate on God's word on a regular basis?

....

....

....

....

DISCUSS IT TOGETHER

Allow your study partner to share what kind of rhythm he/she has established with God's word and how the Bible is the anchor and final authority of evaluating truth.

THE HOLY SPIRIT EMPOWERS YOU AND IS WITH YOU

Some people love to read and study the Bible and seek spiritual growth primarily through interaction with Scripture. Others have a major focus on living in the power of the Holy Spirit, seeking and utilizing his gifts, and discerning his promptings and direction intuitively. In other words, some groups place a higher emphasis on the Word, while others place the emphasis on the Spirit. Jesus, however, modeled and taught the need to be a person of both Word and Spirit. Dependence and sensitivity to the Spirit complements a dedication to Scripture.

6. Read John 14:16-17. What does Jesus promise regarding the Holy Spirit?

....
....
....

7. According to Matthew 3:16-4:1, Jesus began his public ministry by being anointed and led by the Holy Spirit. What does this say to you regarding the role of the Spirit in your life?

....
....
....
....
....
....

Personal Story from Author:

It has only been in the last few years that I have come to better understand the role of the Holy Spirit in my life. I tend to rely on my own human abilities for most things, and I am by nature more of a logical "thinker-type." I have always placed a high priority on knowing the Bible. I know God has blessed this pursuit and has blessed me with my human abilities, but he has also shown me more recently the importance of being led and empowered by the Spirit.

The other day, I felt like I sensed a "prompting" from the Holy Spirit to find a specific person he brought to mind and pray for him. My natural inclination would be to let that thought pass by and not do anything with it. Instead, I found the person and asked if I could lay hands on him and pray for his healing. It felt uncomfortable at first, but afterwards, the person told me how much it meant to him that I would do that without him even asking me.

I am also much more open than I used to be when it comes to practicing all of the gifts of the Spirit according to 1 Cor 12. It has been exciting to see God stretch me in ways that I have not been stretched. I still have a long ways to go in my pursuit of living in the power of the Spirit, but I am becoming much closer to being a man of both Word and Spirit.

Copy the following passages down and notice the connection between the Word and the Spirit.

8. Acts 4:31

....

....

....

9. Ephesians 6:17-18

....

....

....

As we live for Jesus and engage in his mission, there is an enemy that is working against us. The more we attempt to live for God, the more intense the battle becomes. This is a spiritual battle, and it will require greater dependence on the power and leading of God's Spirit.

10. Have you ever felt prompted by the Spirit to do something for someone but didn't do it? In what ways do you think you can become more sensitive to the leading and direction of the Holy Spirit?

....

....

BALANCING IDENTITY AND ACTIVITY

One of the challenges all believers face is the "Christian list" syndrome. Oftentimes, shortly after someone makes a decision to repent and place faith in Jesus, they are given a list of "do's and don'ts." Some common items on the "do" list are: go to church every week, read the Bible regularly, give 10% of your income to the church, serve in a church ministry, reach out to others, help the homeless, give to the poor, participate in Bible studies, go on at least one mission trip per year, show hospitality, etc. All of these things are important and great practices. However, for some, following Jesus ends up being an exhausting exercise in checking items off the list.

Now, our faith certainly should affect the way we live our lives. Jesus made that clear when he said, "If you love me, you will obey my teaching" (John 14:15). Also, James (one of the New Testament authors) reminds his readers that they must be "doers" of the Word and not just "hearers" (James 1:23). At the same time, however, we need to recognize that our "good deeds" don't ever earn us favor with God.

11. Read Luke 10:38-42. What is Jesus teaching in this passage?

Living for Jesus is not a sprint. It is a marathon that is moving in a direction of life. It is just as much about resting in God's love and our identity as his sons and daughters as it is about doing good deeds. There is a rhythm to the Christian life that requires a balance of being and doing, resting and working, identity and activity. Coming to terms with this rhythm will help us avoid the temptation of slipping into either performance or laziness in our relationship with God.

DISCUSS IT TOGETHER

How do you think you can avoid the "Christian list" syndrome? Allow your study partner to share how he/she balances identity and activity.

MENTORING AND BEING MENTORED

We all need the influence of someone who is spiritually further down the road than we are. Likewise, we all need to invest in someone who is not as spiritually mature as we are.

12. Read I Cor. 4:16, 11:1; Heb. 13:7 What are these verses teaching?

....

....

....

....

....

Everyone needs a "Paul" in their life, a mentor or discipler who can encourage and challenge us. While God uses a variety of ways to help us grow, interacting with someone that we respect and want to be more like is one of the most powerful avenues to spiritual maturity. Jesus knew the impact of modeling and mentoring, which is why he mentored twelve men to be his apostles. They followed Jesus' example and then in turn mentored others who followed their example. The way Paul put it was

"Imitate me as I imitate Christ" (1 Cor 11:1).
When seeking out a mentor it is not necessary to formally ask someone, "Will you be my mentor?" Informal, mentor-like relationships are often best. Seek out those you respect and would like to be more like, and look for ways to spend time with them. They may not even know they are mentoring you, but you will be learning by simply watching them and following their example.

Personal Story from Author:
From the moment I came to Christ, I have always sought out people who are further down the road in an area than me. When I was younger, these leaders were always older than I was. I even lived in the homes of leaders of my church. As I have gotten older, some of the people I respect and want to learn from are younger than I am. Any time I see someone who is spiritually mature and has qualities I know I want to develop, I look for ways to spend time with that person and ask lots of questions. The mentors God has given me over the years have made a big contribution to my growth and have been instrumental in me becoming the person I am today.

13. What are some names that come to mind as you think about people you would like to spend more time with for the purpose of growing spiritually?

....
....
....
....

Again, it is not necessary to formally ask them to "mentor" you. Just pursue them and look for ways to spend time with them.

While it is important to have someone you are trying to follow, it is also important to be investing in someone you can impact as well. We need a "Paul" to encourage and challenge us, but we also need a "Timothy" to encourage and challenge.

14. Copy Philippians 2:22.
....
....

....

....

Paul mentored Timothy and invested in him. Even though Timothy was young (I Tim. 4:12), Paul saw great potential in him. Sometimes we think we have so far to go spiritually that there is no one we could help. But just like there are always people who are further along than us, there are also always people who are not as far as we are. Spiritual maturity is more relevant than physical age in this regard. It is important early in one's spiritual journey to create a lifestyle of investing in others.

15. What are the names of some people you could invest in and serve as an example?

....

....

....

....

BECOMING A PART OF A COMMUNITY ON MISSION

As we have seen throughout this book, God is building a family on the earth who will represent him and advance his mission in the world. This was never meant to be done alone. It is to be done within the framework of relationship and community. Becoming a part of a local community of believers (a "church") is part of this process. Finding a community of Jesus-followers who love God, love one another, and go out and love the world is an important part of anyone's spiritual journey.

Many people in our culture have some kind of affiliation with a local church. Because of this, it is important to distinguish the difference between attending services at a local church and becoming a part of a vibrant community of believers who are actively bringing heaven to earth. Often people think that attending a church service on Sundays is the extent of what it means to be involved with other believers in church life. However, as we have seen in this study, simply being religious or even a "church-goer" is not what God wants from us. Attending church services is important for many reasons, but it is only a small part of what it means to be a family on mission.

DISCUSS IT TOGETHER

Discuss with your study partner the difference between "church attendance" and living out Jesus' mission together with a community of believers. What steps can you take to find this kind of "community on mission?"

16. Read Acts 2:38-47. What are a few observations you have from the passage?

....
....
....
....
....
....

In this passage three thousand people believe in Jesus. The first thing they did is get baptized. Being baptized represents spiritual cleansing and the decision to die with Christ to an old life and rise with Christ to a new one. It marks a new beginning with God.

Read the following passages on baptism: Mark 16:15-16, Matthew 28:19, Acts 8:12, 16:33-34, 18:8, 22:16.

After believing and being baptized, they met together regularly, devoting themselves to biblical teaching, fellowship with other believers, communion, meeting one another's needs, exercising spiritual gifts, reaching out to the lost, meeting as large groups in the Temple, and meeting as smaller groups in homes. As all of this was occurring, the church at large was growing and spreading. Believers gathered together in pockets all over their city and joined in God's mission together. They became several different communities of mission.

17. What questions do you have regarding the practice of baptism?

....
....
....
....
....

CHAPTER SUMMARY

Living for Jesus and becoming engaged in his mission means we will live differently than those who don't know Jesus. Our priorities, goals, and lifestyles will be different. However, it can be easy to slip into a performance mentality, where we live by a list of do's and don'ts instead of trusting the Spirit day by day. God, however, doesn't want us to follow religious rules; he wants us to live out a relationship with him. A regular diet of the Bible and sensitivity to the Spirit will set us on the right course and guide our path.

Relationships will also help us ground our faith in God's family. Being a part of a church family that is seeking to live out God's mission for the world is a source of great encouragement and empowerment. Investing in others along the way and following the example of key mentors are part of an ongoing lifestyle of following Jesus. This is a practice that dates back to the first apostles themselves. We are all both disciples and disciplers.

Hopefully this study has given you a solid foundation upon which you can grow. God has given you a mission: his mission, the greatest mission in the world. Go and live out your identity and destiny as you follow the Father, Son, and Holy Spirit in community with others!

"After they prayed, the place where they were meeting was shaken. And they were all filled with the Holy Spirit and spoke the word of God boldly" (Acts 4:31).

As an encouragement for you to look back on, perhaps you would want to write out a prayer on the lines below telling God what this study has meant to you, what you have learned, what your study partner has meant to you, and how you plan to live your life from this day forward.

QUESTIONS OR JOURNAL REFLECTIONS